Underhill's Licensing Guide

Eleventh edition

Simon Mehigan
Barrister

and

Lawrence Stevens
Solicitor

LONGMAN

3143   © Longman Group UK Ltd 1991

ISBN 0 85121 528 X

Published by
Longman Law, Tax and Finance
Longman Group UK Ltd
21–27 Lamb's Conduit Street, London WC1N 3NJ

Associated Offices
Australia, Hong Kong, Malaysia, Singapore, USA

First edition 1956
Eleventh edition 1991

A CIP catalogue record for this book is available from the British Library.

Printed in Great Britain by Mackays of Chatham

Contents

Abbreviations

BGLA63	The Betting, Gaming and Lotteries Act 1963
LA64	The Licensing Act 1964
GA68	The Gaming Act 1968
GCLR69	The Gaming Clubs (Licensing) Regulations 1969 (SI No 1110)
LAA	The Lotteries and Amusements Act 1976
LA88	The Licensing Act 1988

Preface to the Eleventh Edition

In this edition we have not only updated the text, so far as changes in the law are concerned, but have added a chapter (Chapter 7) on applications to the Divisional Court and we have inserted a number of practical points the knowledge of which can only otherwise be gained by experience.

SIMON MEHIGAN

5 Paper Buildings
Temple
LONDON
EC4

June 1991

LAWRENCE STEVENS

Vallance Lickfolds
89 Kingsway
LONDON
WC2

Table of Cases

Table of Statutes

Table of Statutory Instruments

Chapter 1

Liquor Licensing: General

By s 160 of the LA64 it is in general an offence to sell by retail intoxicating liquor without a 'justices' licence'. This means a licence granted by the licensing justices for the licensing district concerned. A retail dealer does not require an excise licence to authorise his sales: the justices' licence alone is sufficient.

Intoxicating liquor is defined in s 201 of the LA64 as follows:

"intoxicating liquor" means spirits, wine, beer, cider, and any other fermented, distilled or spiritous liquor but does not include—

(1) any liquor which, whether made on the premises of a brewer for sale or elsewhere, is found on analysis of a sample thereof at any time to be of an original gravity not exceeding 1016° and of a strength not exceeding 1.2 per cent;
(2) perfumes;
(3) flavouring essences recognised by the Commissioners of Customs and Excise as not being intended for consumption as or with dutiable alcoholic liquor;
(4) spirits, wine or made-wine so medicated as to be, in the opinion of the Commissioners, intended for use as a medicine and not as a beverage.

Angostura bitters are excluded from this definition by the Finance Act 1970.

Note

(1) Under s 1(1) of the Licensing (Retail Sales) Act 'Sale by retail' means a sale of intoxicating liquor at any one time to any one person except where the sale is—

(*a*) to a trader for the purposes of his trade;
(*b*) to a registered club for the purposes of the club;
(*c*) to any canteen or mess;
(*d*) to the holder of an occasional permission within the meaning of the Licensing (Occasional Permissions) Act

1

1983 for the purposes of sales authorised by that permission; or

(*e*) of not less than the following quantities—

(i) in the case of spirits, wine or made-wine, nine litres or one case; or

(ii) in the case of beer or cider, twenty litres or two cases,

and is made from premises owned by the vendor, or occupied by him under a lease to which the provisions of Part 2 of the Landlord and Tenant Act 1954 apply.

Made-wine means any liquor obtained from the alcoholic fermentation of any substance or by mixing a liquor so obtained with any other liquor or substance, but excluding wine, beer, black beer, spirits or cider.

A case means one dozen units each consisting of a container holding not less than sixty-five nor more than eighty centilitres, or the equivalent of that number of such units, made up wholly or partly of containers of a larger or smaller size (Alcoholic Liquor Duties Act 1979, s 4).

(2) Manufacturers also require licences, but this book is principally concerned with retailers' licences.

(3) The Vice-Chancellor of the University of Cambridge still retains the ancient privilege of granting on- and off-licences to sell wine in Cambridge (see LA64, s 199(*a*)).

1 Disqualification for licence

The following persons are disqualified from holding a justices' licence:

(1) a sheriff's officer or officer executing the legal process of any court (LA64, s 9);

(2) a person convicted of forging a justices' licence or making use of a forged justices' licence knowing it to be such (LA64, s 9);

(3) a person convicted of permitting to be a brothel premises for which at the time of the conviction he held a justices' licence (LA64, s 9);

(4) any person who is convicted of selling or exposing for sale by retail any liquor without holding a justices' licence, or, being the holder of such a licence, is convicted of selling or exposing for sale by retail any liquor except at the place for which the licence authorises its sale, may be ordered to be disqualified from holding a justices' licence:

(a) on a second conviction for a period not exceeding five years;

(b) on a third or subsequent conviction for any term of years or for life (LA64, s 160).

Note

(1) The justices also have power in certain cases to make disqualification orders for restaurant licences, residential licences and restaurant and residential licences (see Chapter 2).

(2) Premises are disqualified for receiving a justices' licence where they are situated on land acquired or appropriated for 'special roads'. Special roads are highways provided for under the Highways Act 1980, eg motorways (LA64, s 9).

(3) Premises which are primarily used as a garage, ie for the retail of petrol or derv or the sale/maintenance of motor vehicles, are now disqualified from receiving a justices' licence (LA64, s 9(4A) and (4B) as inserted by LA88, s 10). However, this change does not affect garage premises for which prior to 22 August 1988 there was a justices' licence so long as the licence does not lapse.

2 Justices' licences (LA64, ss 1–4)

Justices' licences are granted by the licensing justices at their 'Licensing Sessions'. This term is used to cover the licensing justices' General Annual Licensing Meeting (often called Brewster Sessions) and the intervening transfer sessions. The licensing justices are a committee of the ordinary justices of the peace to whom special tasks in connection with licensing have been assigned.

There are two main kinds of justices' licence: on-licences and off-licences.

On-licences are of five kinds depending on the liquor which the licence allows to be sold:

(1) intoxicating liquor of all descriptions;
(2) beer, cider and wine only;
(3) beer and cider only;
(4) cider only;
(5) wine only.

Off-licences are of two kinds, also depending on the type of liquor concerned:

(1) intoxicating liquor of all descriptions;
(2) beer, cider and wine only.

Note

An applicant for a licence for an ordinary public house will apply for a licence to sell 'intoxicating liquor of all descriptions, either on or off the premises'. This is often called a 'full on-licence' or 'publican's licence'. An on-licence normally authorises sale for consumption either on or off the premises. If it is desired to permit on-sales only, a condition (see **3** below) may be attached to the licence to this effect.

3 Licensing procedure (LA64, Sched 1)

The licensing justices for each district must hold a General Annual Licensing Meeting and not less than four transfer sessions in the twelve months beginning with February every year. The licensing sessions are held at as nearly regular intervals as may be. Brewster Sessions (the popular name for the General Annual Licensing Meeting) are held in the first fortnight of February.

The clerk to the justices is required to advertise the time and place for holding any licensing sessions in a newspaper circulating in the district, and to send notice of it:

(1) to every member of the licensing committee (ie the justices);

(2) to every holder of a justices' licence in the district;

(3) to every person who gives or has given the clerk notice of intention to apply for a licence at the sessions;

(4) to the chief officer of police for the police area or each of the police areas in which the district or any part of it is situated. As to 'chief officer of police' see LA64, s 201(4) and below, where the meaning of the phrase is set out.

(a) Notices (LA64, Sched 2)

An applicant at a licensing sessions for the grant of a new justices' licence or for the ordinary or special removal or transfer of a justices' licence must give the *notices* below.

(By s 197 of the LA64, any notice under the Act may be served by post; accordingly the presumptions in s 7 of the Interpretation Act 1978 will apply to prove service in the absence of contrary evidence. In practice registered or recorded delivery post is generally used for the service of such notices in order that proof of service may be readily available or evidence is called to prove addressing, pre-paying and posting.)

(1) Not less than twenty-one days before the day of the licensing sessions he must give notice in writing to the clerk to the justices, the chief officer of police and the proper local authority

and, in certain cases, to the relevant fire authority (see below).

(2) In the case of a transfer he must give the like notice to the holder of the licence (if any) and in the case of a removal he must give the like notice to the registered owner of the premises from which it is sought to remove the licence, and the holder of the licence (if any), unless he is also the applicant.

(3) Except in the case of a transfer he must:

(a) not more than twenty-eight days before the day of the sessions display notice of the application for a period of seven days in a place where it can conveniently be read by the public on or near the premises to be licensed (or, in the case of an application for a provisional grant, on or near the proposed site of the premises); and

(b) not more than twenty-eight days nor less than fourteen days before the day of the licensing sessions (and, if the justices so require, on some day or days outside that period but within such other period as they may require) advertise notice of the application in a newspaper circulating in the place where the premises to be licensed are situated. (It need not be a local newspaper.)

An applicant at a transfer sessions for the renewal of a justices' licence must, not less than twenty-one days before the day of the sessions, give notice in writing to the clerk to the licensing justices, the chief officer of police and the proper local authority.

Note

In the case of a notice which must be given 'not less than' a number of days it is clear that the exact number of days must pass between service and the hearing, ie the days of service and hearing are not included.

With the notice given to the clerk to the justices there must be deposited a *plan* of the premises to be licensed if the application is:

(1) for the grant of a new justices' on-licence or of an ordinary removal of a justices' on-licence; or

(2) for the provisional grant of a new justices' off-licence or for the ordinary removal of a justices' off-licence.

The Licensing Act does not specify with precision exactly how the plans should be prepared but there are often local regulations as to colouring and scale and these will be revealed by local enquiry. For example, many licensing justices require plans to be coloured in such a way that the areas where intoxicating liquors are intended to be sold or consumed are marked in a particular colour (often pink), with other facilities such as kitchens, lavatories etc having different colours.

Note, however, that this does not apply to some applications for provisional grants where in certain cases 'outline plans' are allowed (see **6** below).

All the above notices must:

(1) be signed by the applicant or his agent;
(2) state the applicant's name and address and, except in the case of a removal of a licence held by him or of a renewal, his trade or calling during the six months preceding the giving of the notice;
(3) state the situation of the premises to be licensed and, in the case of a removal, the premises from which it is sought to remove the licence;
(4) in the case of a new licence, state the kind of licence for which application is to be made.

The notice to the local authority must be given:

(1) if the premises are outside Greater London, to the proper officer of the district council; and
(2) if the premises are in a parish, to the proper officer of the parish council, or, where there is no parish council, to the chairman of the parish meeting;
(3) if the premises are in a community where there is a community council, to the proper officer of that council; and
(4) if the premises are inside Greater London, by virtue of para 6(6) of Sched 29 to the Local Government Act 1972 notice must also be given to the proper officer of the local authority, usually the clerk to the relevant London borough council or in the City of London, the Clerk to the Common Council. The 'proper officer' is one appointed by the council for that purpose.

The notice to the chief officer of police must be given:

(1) if the premises to which the notice relates (ie in the case of an application for a licence, the premises to be licensed) are in the City of London, to the Commissioner of Police for the City;
(2) if the premises are in the Metropolitan Police District, to the Commissioner of Police of the Metropolis;
(3) if the premises are in any other police area, to the chief constable of that area (LA64, s 201(4)).

With the notice given to the Chief Officer of Police it is convenient to provide details of the applicant for the licence and in particular his address and occupation over the last year, his experience and whether or not he has any convictions. Sometimes either the police or the justices like to see written references on behalf of the applicant.

The notice to be given to the local authority must also be given, in the case of a new licence or a removal, to the authority discharging in the area the functions of a fire authority under the Fire Services Act 1947. (In Greater London this is the London Fire and Civil Defence Authority.)

The clerk to the justices must keep for all sessions a list of the persons giving notice of their intention to apply for the grant of a licence, and the list must show:

(*a*) the applicant's name and address;
(*b*) the nature of the application;
(*c*) the situation of the premises to be licensed.

For the fourteen days preceding the sessions the list must be open to inspection at all reasonable times by any person on payment of the appropriate fee (if any) and by a Customs and Excise representative.

Note

Applicants will usually be required to prove all the above notices, and evidence should be available. Frequently they are proved by certificates of posting or by a representative of the applicant's solicitors stating that he posted the notices, or by the production of acknowledgements from the various recipients.

If an applicant for the grant of a justices' licence has, through inadvertence or misadventure, failed to comply with the rules about giving notice, the justices may, on such terms as they think fit, postpone consideration of the application. These terms may be that all notices are to be re-served, re-displayed and re-advertised. If on the postponed consideration they are satisfied that any terms so imposed have been complied with, they may deal with the application as if the applicant had complied with the rules. The applicant on the consideration of an application for a licence must, if required by the justices, attend in person. In the case of a renewal, however, the applicant is not required to attend unless objection is made to the renewal. The justices may postpone consideration of an application until the applicant attends.

A specimen form of application for a new licence is shown at Appendix 1. Licensing justices frequently wish to *inspect* premises that are to be licensed, and should of course be given every facility for this.

Many licensing areas issue guidelines dealing with local procedural matters such as requirements relating to plans, documents to be provided, method of proving service of notices and length of notice where not laid down by statute: eg notice of application for a final order or for consent under s 20.

(b) The hearing of licensing applications

The procedure to be followed when the grant of a new licence is under consideration varies slightly from place to place. A usual form of procedure is as follows:

The clerk calls on the application, shortly stating its nature. He enquires whether there are any objectors, taking down the names and addresses of any who answer.

The applicant's counsel or solicitor (or the applicant in person) 'opens' his case. Evidence in support of it is then given on oath by the applicant and any witnesses whom he may call. The applicant and his witnesses are then cross-examined by any objector or by counsel or solicitor on the objector's behalf.

Any objector may then address the meeting in person or by counsel or solicitor and call evidence on oath. The objector, if he gives evidence, and his witnesses (if any) may be cross-examined by the applicant or his counsel or solicitor.

At the conclusion of the evidence the objector (or his representative) addresses the justices, and the applicant (or his representative) replies if he has not already addressed the justices.

(c) Objectors

The justices may hear any objectors who wish to raise objections to the grant of the new licence. Objectors need give no notice of their intention to oppose (cf the position regarding objectors to a renewal). Any member of the public may oppose the grant of a new licence on public grounds, apart from any private interest (eg as a trade competitor) which he may have in the matter.

(d) The justices' discretion

Under s 3(1) of the LA64 the justices have a general discretion to grant a licence to any person whom they think fit and proper. The Act nowhere lays down a requirement to prove 'need' or 'demand', but the justices generally require such need to be established by evidence.

Where justices require need or demand to be established they will expect to have produced to them evidence in support of this factor. The attitude and practice of licensing justices varies a great deal but where proof of demand is required consideration can be given to support by way of local witnesses, analysis of the facilities in the area, movements in population and changes in the area. Sometimes it is also possible to indicate that the number of facilities has for some reason declined or that in some way these facilities are no longer adequate for current requirements.

It is often the case that the court will require maps to be produced to show the facilities in a quarter of a mile or half a mile radius from the relevant premises. Enquiries should always be made of the clerk to the licensing justices to ascertain the particular local requirements.

By s 4(2) of the LA64 the justices may not grant a new on-licence for premises unless the premises are in their opinion 'structurally adapted' to the class of licence required.

(e) Conditions

When granting a new on-licence (other than one for the sale of wine alone) the justices may attach to it such conditions governing the tenure of the licence and any other matters as they think proper in the interests of the public (LA64, s 4(1)). For instance they may limit the sale of liquor to certain parts of the premises, such as requiring a supermarket to segregate the area in which liquor is sold from the remainder of the premises ('a shop within a shop'), or may require some exit to be kept unobstructed.

A variety of conditions may be imposed upon licences depending upon the circumstances.

It would not be possible to set out all the different kinds of conditions which might be imposed but the following are some illustrations—

Hotels: These may be subject to the conditions provided for residential or restaurant and residential licences under s 94. Some hotels have unrestricted licences and some have conditions which fall between the two such as—
  (1) No off sales.
  (2) No direct access from the street to any bar.
  (3) No external advertisement of a licensed bar.

Clubs:
  (1) Intoxicating liquor shall not be sold or supplied otherwise than to members of the club meeting at the premises for consumption by such members and their bona fide guests.
  (2) No person shall be admitted to membership of the club without an interval of at least two days between nomination or application for membership and admission. The names and

addresses of persons who are applying must be prominently displayed in the club premises in a part frequented by the members for at least two days before admission to membership.
(3) No off sales.

There is a right of appeal to the Crown Court against the imposition of any conditions considered to be too onerous.

Such 'optional' conditions, once attached to a licence, may not be varied; if it is wished to remove them, a new licence must be applied for. Breach of certain conditions may lead to a prosecution under LA64, s 161 and breach of any condition will risk a refusal to renew the licence or, since 1 March 1989, the revocation of the licence (LA64, s 20A). Optional conditions attached to an on-licence are to be distinguished from the 'statutory' conditions imposed by virtue of various provisions of the LA64 (eg the conditions attached to Part IV licences for restaurants etc: LA64, s 94).

(f) Undertakings

Since the justices have no power to impose conditions when granting off-licences, 'undertakings' have sometimes been asked for from the applicant for such a licence; eg an undertaking to sell a particular type of liquor only. The legality of this practice is doubtful, but it seems that 'non-legally binding assurances' may be required by the justices in some cases. If such an 'assurance' is given and not complied with, the licence holder will not be exposed to prosecution; but the non-compliance may lead to the renewal of a licence being refused.

Even in the case of on-licences, the justices sometimes require undertakings to be given where the subject matter is not thought appropriate to be dealt with by way of a condition on the licence. For example an undertaking might be required that an application be made to add an additional licence holder within a specific period, or that work required by the local authority or the fire brigade is completed within a specified time. This practice can be helpful in enabling a decision to be made earlier than would perhaps otherwise be the case.

(g) Costs

On the hearing of an application under the LA64 relating to licensed premises the licensing justices may make such order as they think just and reasonable for the payment of costs to the applicant by any person opposing the application or by the applicant to any such person.

The High Court have, however, held that where the police unsuccessfully opposed the renewal of a licence they should not be ordered to pay costs if they had acted fairly and in line with their duty.

4 Permitted hours

(a) General licensing hours

It is a criminal offence to sell intoxicating liquor outside permitted hours (LA64, s 59). What constitutes permitted hours has been significantly changed in amendments to LA64, s 60 made by LA88, s 1. Now permitted hours in premises with a justices' on-licence are as follows:

(1) On weekdays (other than Christmas Day or Good Friday) 11 am–11 pm. *Note*: There is no longer any distinction between London and elsewhere.

(2) On Sundays, Christmas Day and Good Friday 12 noon to 10.30 pm with a break of four hours beginning at 3 pm.

Under s 60(4), as amended, the hours referred to in (1) above may be modified if the licensing justices are satisfied that the requirements of the district make it desirable that drinking should start at 10 am. See also s 61 in respect of the exercise of the power under s 60(4) which states that any application under s 60(4) must be made to the Brewster Sessions.

Note

General 'drinking up' time has been extended from ten to twenty minutes (LA64, s 63(1)(*a*), as amended by LA88, s 2), but the thirty minutes drinking up time applicable where customers are taking a meal at the premises and where liquor was supplied for consumption as an ancillary to a meal remains the same. Permitted hours in off-licences on weekdays other than Christmas Day or Good Friday begin at 8 am (LA64, s 60(6), as amended by LA88, s 1(4)).

(b) Additions to permitted hours

As these usually, although not always, concern restaurant premises, they are set out in Chapter 2.

(c) Restrictions of permitted hours

(1) *Restriction orders* (LA64, ss 67A–D) Although the LA88 has increased the number of permitted hours as stated above provision is also made for restricting those hours in certain cases. Under LA64, ss 67A–D (which are inserted by LA88, s 3) the main effect of a

restriction order is that it may prevent the sale of liquor from 2.30 pm–5.30pm or any part thereof. A restriction order cannot apply in the case of an off-licence or an occasional licence. An application for a restriction order may only be made by a chief officer of police, by or on behalf of a person living or carrying on a business in the neighbourhood or by a person in charge of an educational establishment in the neighbourhood. The grounds on which an order can be made are:

(1) that it is desirable to avoid or reduce any disturbance of or annoyance to—

    (*a*) persons living or working in the neighbourhood,

    (*b*) customers or clients of any business in the neighbourhood, or

    (*c*) persons attending, or in charge of persons attending, any educational establishment in the neighbourhood,

    due to the use of the premises or part of the premises; or

(2) that it is desirable to avoid or reduce the occurrence of disorderly conduct in the premises, or the occurrence in the vicinity of the premises of disorderly conduct on the part of persons resorting to the premises.

A restriction order has effect for a maximum of twelve months: when it expires application has to be made for a new one. It is made by licensing justices in the case of licensed premises and by a magistrates' court in the case of a registered club.

Section 67B makes provision for appeals to the Crown Court against the granting of a restriction order or as to its terms, but only in the case of the holder of a licence, ie it appears that an unsuccessful applicant for such an order cannot appeal. This is also apparent from LA64, s 21(1) (*ee*) (as substituted by LA88, Sched 3, para 3). The respondents are the applicant for the order and the justices. If an appeal is brought then the restriction order is suspended until it is disposed of unless the justices or Crown Court order otherwise.

Note

It appears that for the suspension to operate an appeal must actually be brought. There is no provision that suspension exists in any event during the twenty-one day appeal period.

Under s 67C, once a restriction order is in force an application can be made by the licence holder in order to have the order revoked or varied. No such application can be made within six months of the date on which the order came into force, nor it seems, where a previous application to revoke/vary has been made.

The procedure which applies to applications under s 67A and s 67C is to be found in Sched 8A to the LA64 (as inserted by LA88, Sched 2). In the case of any application relating to a restriction order, notice in writing (specifying the grounds of the application in general terms) must be given to the clerk to the licensing justices not later than twenty-one days before the relevant licensing sessions. In the case of an application for the making of such an order, notice should in most cases also be given to the holder of the justices' licence. In the case of an application for the variation or revocation of an order, notice should also be given to the chief officer of police, and to the person on whose application the order was made.

There is a different procedure relevant to objections to applications for variation or revocation. Under this a person intending to oppose an application for the variation or revocation of a restriction order shall give not later than seven days before the relevant licensing session written notice specifying in general terms the grounds of opposition to the applicant. Where the formalities of notice giving are not complied with, the justices may adjourn the application and hear it on another occasion.

Note

Evidence given on an application to licensing justices for the making, variation or revocation of a restriction order must be on oath.

Similar provisions are made in the case of registered clubs for hearing before magistrates.

(2) *Sporting events* Under the Sporting Events (Control of Alcohol etc) Act 1985 special provision is made for licensing hours within sports grounds. The Act has the effect of restricting the permitted hours but there is provision for an application to be made to a magistrates court enabling intoxicating liquor to be sold, supplied or consumed in a part of the premises if the event cannot be directly viewed from that point. The Act only applies at the moment to association football.

(3) *Six-day licences: early-closing licences* When an application is made for the grant of a new on-licence or for the transfer, removal or renewal of such a licence, the justices must insert, if the applicant requests it, a condition that there shall be no permitted hours on Sundays in the premises concerned or that the permitted hours shall end one hour earlier in the evening than those fixed under the ordinary provisions for such hours.

If the former condition is inserted, the licence is called a six-day licence. If the latter condition is inserted, it is called an early-closing licence (LA64, s 65).

The justices must revoke the six-day or early-closing condition on an application by the licence holder requesting them to do so.

The only object of obtaining a six-day, early-closing or seasonal licence (see below) would appear to be to prevent the licence holder being open to criticism (or possibly to objections to the renewal of his licence on the ground of a lack of public demand) if he habitually closes his premises early, or on Sundays, or for substantial periods of the year. A licence holder is not, of course, obliged to keep his premises open for the whole of the 'permitted hours'.

(4) *Seasonal licences* Any person applying for an on-licence (whether a new licence or not) may request that a condition be inserted that during such part or parts of the year as are specified there shall be no permitted hours (eg at a seaside hotel which is closed in the winter). Such a request may also be made by a licence holder at any licensing sessions. If the justices are satisfied that the requirements of the district make it desirable they may insert the condition, and the licence is then a 'seasonal licence'. The condition may be varied or revoked on application by the holder, or on the renewal, transfer or removal of the licence at the applicant's request (LA64, s 64).

5 Duration of licences

(a) The usual position (LA64, s 26)

Radical changes to the duration of licences have been introduced by LA88, s 11(1) which amends LA64, s 26. If a justices' licence has been granted since 4 January 1989, but before 5 April 1989, it has effect from the time of grant until 4 April 1992. If granted after 4 April 1989 it has effect until the expiry of the 'current licensing period', ie a period of three years from 5 April 1989 or any three-year period thereafter. If, however, it is granted in the last three months of that period, ie from 5 January–4 April 1992 it has effect until April 1995. Note that the grant is superseded by the coming into force of a licence granted by way of renewal, transfer or removal.

A justices' licence granted by way of transfer or removal may be granted to have effect from a time specified in the grant (not being earlier, when it is granted before the coming into force of the licence transferred or removed, than the time of the coming into force of that licence).

(b) Possible or pending appeals (LA64, s 27)

The general position regarding appeals is to be found at **22** below, but it is necessary at this stage to consider the effect of an appeal on the duration of a licence.

Where, on application to the licensing justices for the grant of a new justices' licence or for the grant of a licence by way of ordinary removal of a justices' licence, an objector appears before the licensing justices and opposes the grant, but the justices grant the licence, special rules apply, as follows:

(1) until the expiration of the time for bringing an appeal against the grant (ie twenty-one days), and, if such an appeal is brought, until the appeal has been disposed of:

   (*a*) the licence granted does not come into force;

   (*b*) in the case of an ordinary removal the licence which it is sought to remove, if it is in force at the time of the grant, does not expire (unless the justices order the contrary);

(2) if on appeal the grant is confirmed or if the appeal is abandoned, the time when the appeal is disposed of is substituted for the time of the grant for the purpose of determining the period for which the licence is to have effect, and the Crown Court must (if need be) amend the licence accordingly:

(3) if there is an appeal against the grant of an ordinary removal, and the licence which it is sought to remove is in force on the day when the notice of appeal is given to the applicant for the removal, then:

   (*a*) he may within seven days of that day give notice in writing to the proper officer of the Crown Court of his desire that the expiration of that licence be postponed for a specified period (not exceeding three weeks) after the appeal is disposed of, and if he does so, the licence does not expire until the expiration of the period;

   (*b*) whether or not he gives such a notice, the Crown Court, if it confirms the grant and if he so requests, may by its order direct that the new licence shall not come into force and the old one shall not expire for such a further period as it thinks fit;

   (*c*) if the Crown Court refuses to confirm the grant, and at the time of its decision it is too late to renew that licence at the Brewster Sessions at which it was due for renewal, then:

      (i) the holder of the licence is treated as having had reasonable cause for not applying for renewal at that meeting, and the licence may be renewed at a transfer sessions accordingly; and

(ii) if notice has been given by the applicant and within the period for which the licence is continued in force notice is given to the clerk to the justices of an application for the renewal of the licence at the first licensing sessions held not less than twenty-one days after the notice is given, the licence does not expire until the application is disposed of or those sessions end without it being made.

Note

Where the holder of a justices' licence gives notice of appeal against a refusal by the licensing justices to renew that licence, or a decision by them to revoke it (on the power to revoke, which came into existence on 1 March 1989, see below) the justices or Crown Court may, on such conditions as they think fit, order that the licence shall continue in force until the determination of the appeal notwithstanding that the appeal is not determined until after the date when the licence would otherwise cease to have effect (LA64, s 21(4)). Further under LA64, s 23(4), from 1 March 1989, where the Crown Court allows an appeal against the revocation of a justices' licence which has been continued in force under s 21(4), it may order that the licence shall further continue in force until the date of the next licensing sessions for the district in which the licence is granted.

The new s 20A(5) (as inserted by LA88, s 12(1)), which comes into force on 1 March 1989, makes it clear that a decision to revoke a justices' licence has no effect until the expiry of the twenty-one days time for appealing against the decision or if the decision is appealed against, until the appeal is disposed of.

6 Provisional grants (LA64, s 6)

Applications are sometimes made for licences in respect of buildings not yet constructed, or not completed. Any person interested in such premises may apply to the licensing justices for a provisional grant of licence for them. If satisfied with the plans of the building, the justices may make such a grant. Such a provisional grant is ineffective, however, until it is declared final by the licensing justices. The justices will declare it final if satisfied:

(1) that the premises have been completed in accordance with the plans deposited; and

(2) that the holder of the provisional licence is not disqualified from holding a justices' licence and is in all respects a fit and proper person to hold such licence (LA64, s 6(4)).

New provisions (LA64, s 6(4A) and (4B)) make it possible to have a grant finalised by a single licensing justice even before the premises have been completed if it is likely that completion will take place before the date of the next licensing sessions.

On an application for a direction under these provisions the justices will require to be satisfied as to the state and progress of the work before deciding whether to exercise their discretion.

Notwithstanding, however, that they are not satisfied that the premises have been completed in accordance with the original plans the justices will declare the grant final if they are satisfied that the premises have been completed in accordance with the plans as modified, if they have consented to the modifications.

Applications for consent to such modifications may be made at any licensing sessions and the justices may give consent if they consider that the premises will be fit and convenient for their purpose if completed in accordance with the modified plans.

Generally, the plans deposited must be plans of the premises. But for a provisional grant a plan sufficient to identify the site of the premises together with the description of their proposed size and character (with reference in particular to the sale of liquor) may be deposited, and the justices must deal with the application as if the full plans had been deposited and assume that the premises will be fit and convenient. But any provisional grant made in these circumstances becomes ineffective unless 'affirmed' (see below) at licensing sessions held within twelve months of the grant (or where there is an appeal, of the date when the appeal is disposed of: LA64, s 6(5)).

The justices must affirm the provisional grant if satisfied that the premises, if completed in accordance with the full plans deposited, will be fit and convenient for their purpose.

Provisional grants may be made not only where premises are about to be constructed or in the course of construction but also where they are about to be altered or extended or in course of alteration or extension. (As to alterations to licensed premises where a new licence or a removal is not required, see **16** below.)

Provisional grants may be made in respect of both on- and off-licensed premises.

The justices may lay down the amount of notice they require before they declare the grant to be final. This is usually twenty-one days.

No special form of application is required where a provisional grant is sought; the ordinary form (see **3** above and Appendix 1) can be used. However, where the application is for a provisional grant, it is expedient to disclose this on the notice, although not essential to do so.

7 Register of licences (LA64, ss 30,31)

The clerk to the licensing justices is required to keep a register of licences in the licensing district containing:
(1) particulars of justices' licences granted in the district;
(2) the premises for which they were granted;
(3) the names of the owners of the premises;
(4) the names of the holders of the licences.
The clerk is required to enter in the register:
(1) notice of any conviction of the licence holder of an offence committed by him as such;
(2) any forfeiture of a justices' licence granted in the licensing district;
(3) disqualification of any premises;
(4) any other matter relating to the licences on the register (eg any report from an election court as to bribery or treating at an election, in accordance with the Representation of the People Act 1983).

8 Variation of on-licences (LA64, s 37)

The holder of an on-licence may apply at any licensing sessions for it to be varied so as to add to the descriptions of liquor to be sold. The application may also be made on a renewal or transfer at the request of the person applying for the renewal or transfer. The justices must vary the licence as required if satisfied that the application or request is made with the consent of the registered owner.

Where the premises are in a new town, however, the licence may not be varied unless the justices are satisfied that the special committee for the new town have no objection.

Where a licence is varied in this way the justices have power to attach conditions just as if they were granting the varied licence as a new licence, and any conditions attached may be in addition to or in substitution for any previous conditions. There is, however, the same right of appeal against the attachment of any conditions as there is against the refusal of a renewal, and on appeal the Crown Court may make any order for the attachment of any conditions which the justices could have made (LA64, s 21(1)(*f*)).

By virtue of the Licensing (Amendment) Act 1980, s 1(2) this provision for the 'upgrading' of on-licences applies only to those licences which were in force on or before 3 August 1961. This amendment was introduced principally to prevent holders of licences for wine-bars (wine alone licences) in effect compelling the justices to upgrade them to full on-licences. Holders of such licences which were not in force on the above date must, if they wish to upgrade them, apply for a new licence, when objectors may oppose the application.

9 Renewals (LA64, ss 7,193A)

(a) Procedure

Application for renewal of a justices' licence must be made to the Brewster Sessions immediately preceding the end of any licensing period. A justices' licence may not be renewed at a transfer sessions except where the licence was due for renewal at the preceding Brewster Sessions and the justices are satisfied that the applicant had reasonable cause for not applying for renewal at that sessions. If the licence expires through failure to apply for renewal at Brewster Sessions, a subsequent application for a similar licence for the same premises will be treated as an application for renewal if made not later than the next Brewster Sessions and the justices are satisfied that there was reasonable cause for the failure.

Notice of intention to apply for a renewal is normally informal and the applicant should apply by registered post or by recorded delivery service, addressing his letter to the clerk to the justices. But if the applicant intends to apply at transfer sessions he must give written notice not less than twenty-one days before the sessions to the clerk to the licensing justices, the chief officer of police and the local authority (see **3** above).

The clerk to the licensing justices can exercise the power of renewal in the case of unopposed applications unless the justices have directed otherwise or there is a relevant entry in the register of justices' licences or the application is made in conjunction with any other application or request relating to the licence in question.

A person intending to oppose an application for a renewal must give notice in writing of such intention to the applicant and to the clerk to the licensing justices specifying the general grounds of his opposition not later than seven days before Brewster Sessions. If notice has not been so given the justices cannot hear the objection.

The applicant cannot be required to attend in person unless objection is made to the renewal (LA64, Sched 2, para 8).

The justices themselves may raise objection to the renewal of a licence if, for instance, they are not satisfied with the management or conduct of the premises.

(b) Discretion of justices to renew

The discretion of the justices as to the grant of renewals varies according to the type of licence concerned as follows:

(1) *'Old on-licences'*   An 'old on-licence' is one that was in force on 15 August 1904 for the sale of intoxicating liquor, other than wine alone for consumption on the premises.

The justices can only refuse to renew such a licence on any of the following grounds:

(1) that the premises have been ill-conducted or are structurally deficient or structurally unsuitable;
(2) that the applicant is not a fit person to hold the licence;
(3) that the renewal of the licence would be void;
(4) that there has been entered in the register of licences a conviction of bribery or treating made in pursuance of s 168(7) of the Representation of the People Act 1983. (This section provides that when a licence holder is convicted of the election offences of bribery or treating committed on his premises the court shall direct that the conviction be entered in the register of licences.)

There is an appeal to the Crown Court against a refusal to renew.

(2) *'Old beerhouse' licences*   An 'old beerhouse' licence is an on-licence for the sale of beer or cider, with or without wine, which was granted and in force on 15 August 1904 in respect of premises for which a corresponding excise licence was in force on 1 May 1869 (including licences granted by way of renewal of such a licence, whether the licence continues to be held by the same person or has been or may be transferred to any other person).

The justices can only refuse to renew such a licence on any of the following grounds:

(1) that the applicant has failed to produce satisfactory evidence of good character;
(2) that the house or shop to which the application relates or any adjacent house or shop owned or occupied by him is of a disorderly character or frequented by thieves, prostitutes or persons of bad character;
(3) that a licence previously held by the applicant for the sale of wine, spirits, beer or cider has been forfeited for his miscon-

duct; or that he has previously been adjudged for his misconduct disqualified for receiving such a licence or from selling wine, spirits, beer or cider;

(4) that there has been entered in the register of licences a conviction of bribery or treating made in pursuance of s 168(7) of the Representation of the People Act 1983 (see above);

(5) that the applicant is not or the premises are not qualified to be licensed.

There is an appeal to the Crown Court against a refusal to renew.

(3) *Other on-licences* The discretion of the justices as to the renewal of on-licences (other than Part IV licences: see Chapter 2) which are not either 'old beerhouse' licences or 'old on-licences' is absolute. There is, however, an appeal to the Crown Court against a refusal to renew. Where a licence holder gives notice of appeal against a refusal to renew the licence, the justices or the Crown Court may, on such conditions as they think fit, order that the licence shall remain in force until the determination of the appeal, notwithstanding that the appeal is not determined until after the date when the licence would otherwise cease to have effect (LA64, s 21(4)).

(4) Off-licences Subject to an appeal to the Crown Court, the magistrates have a general discretion as to the renewal of off-licences.

Notes

Most ordinary on- and off-licences are renewed, in the absence of objection, without any formal hearing in court.

Under LA64, s 193A (as inserted by LA88, s 13) where an application for the renewal of a justices' licence is made to the Brewster Sessions immediately preceding the expiry of a licensing period, the clerk to the licensing justices may exercise on behalf of the justices their powers of renewal if the application is unopposed, or in a case where the application can only be refused on specified grounds (see above), it is not opposed on a ground on which renewal may be refused. However, the clerk cannot exercise the power to renew if either the justices so direct, or if the application is made in conjunction with any other application or request with respect to the licence sought to be renewed, or there is a 'relevant entry' in the register of justices' licences which relates to the applicant or the premises for which the licence is sought. A relevant entry is one made under LA64, s 31 (see above: it relates to conviction, forfeiture and disqualification) or under the Representation of the People Act 1983 (reports or convictions of bribery or treating).

10 Transfers (LA64, s 8)

Justices' licences may be transferred from one person to another if the justices so allow. Applications for transfers may be made at any licensing sessions. See **3** above for procedure as to transfers.

(a) Grounds for transfer

Transfers can only be granted in the following cases:

(1) Where the holder of the licence has died, to his representative or the new tenant or occupier of the premises.

(2) Where the holder of the licence becomes incapable through illness or other infirmity of carrying on business under the licence, to his assignee or the new tenant or occupier of the premises.

(3) Where the holder of the licence is adjudged bankrupt or a voluntary arrangement is approved under Part VIII of the Insolvency Act 1986, or a trustee is appointed under a deed of arrangement for the benefit of the creditors of the holder of the licence, to his trustee or the new tenant or occupier of the premises.

(4) Where the holder of the licence has, or his representatives have, given up occupation of the premises, to the new tenant or occupier of the premises or the person to whom the representatives or assignees have by sale or otherwise bona fide conveyed or made over their interest in the premises. (*Note* This allows the transfer of a licence where the licence holder or his representatives is or are about to give up occupation. A person occupying the premises for the purpose of carrying on business under the licence is treated as giving up occupation on his giving up the business even if he temporarily remains in occupation of the premises or part of them.)

(5) Where the occupier of the premises, being about to quit them, has wilfully omitted or neglected to apply for renewal of the licence, to the new tenant or occupier of the premises.

(6) Where the owner of licensed premises or some person on his behalf has been granted a protection order (see below), to the owner or person applying on his behalf so long as the application for transfer is made at the first or second licensing sessions after the time when the protection order was granted.

A transfer remains in effect during the currency of the licence, but may be granted before the coming into force of the licence transferred or after it has ceased for any reason to be in force. The justices cannot grant a transfer except to a person who is in their opinion fit and proper.

(b) Justices' discretion

The justices in general have discretion to refuse transfers, but appeal lies to the Crown Court in case of refusal. Transfers of Part IV licences can only be refused on the grounds on which renewals of such licences may be refused (see Chapter 2).

In the case of old on-licences and old beerhouse licences the justices can only refuse a transfer on the grounds on which they can refuse a renewal (see **9** above). But the transfer of an old beerhouse licence can be refused on the further ground that the applicant is not a fit and proper person.

11 Protection orders (LA64, ss 10,11)

Occasion may arise where an authority is required to enable a person to carry on business on licensed premises pending the grant of a transfer at transfer sessions. This authority is conferred by the grant of a protection order, which protects its holder from the penalties for selling without a licence until the transfer of the licence. Such orders are made by the justices acting for the relevant petty sessions area, not by the licensing justices.

The justices have a discretion to grant or refuse the order. If it is granted the protected person can then carry on the business.

Such an order may be granted to anyone to whom a transfer would be granted. It remains in force until the conclusion of the second licensing sessions begun after the date of the order and until any application made at the sessions for a transfer of the licence has been disposed of, but it ceases to have effect before then on the coming into force of a licence granted by way of transfer or removal, or the coming into force of a further protection order.

A protection order may be made for the premises so as to supersede a previous protection order, if the justices are satisfied that the person granted the previous protection order consents to its being superseded, or that he no longer proposes to apply for a transfer of the licences, or is not qualified to do so, or that he is for any reason unable to carry on business under the protection order.

(a) Procedure

Protection orders are not granted by the licensing justices but by the magistrates' court for the petty sessional area in which the licensed premises are situated.

Not less than seven days before the application, the applicant must give notice in writing to the chief officer of police who will normally require details of the applicant's experience and possibly references.

The notice must state his name and address and his trade or calling during the six months preceding the notice.

In an urgent case, the order may be granted if the applicant has given such notice to the police as the justices think reasonable.

(b) Death or bankruptcy of licensee

Where the licensee dies or is adjudged bankrupt or has entered an approved voluntary arrangement, the personal representatives or trustee in bankruptcy or supervisor are in the same position as regards carrying on the business under the licence as if they had been granted a protection order on the death or bankruptcy.

(c) Protection order in case of forfeiture

Where:

(1) a justices' licence for any premises is forfeited (see **13** below) for the first time:

   (a) by virtue of a conviction for making an internal communication between licensed premises and any unlicensed premises;

   (b) by virtue of a second or subsequent conviction for selling or exposing for sale by retail any intoxicating liquor without a licence;

(2) a justices' licence is forfeited by order of a magistrates' court on account of structural alterations in licensed premises being made without the consent of the licensing justices;

(3) a justices' licence is forfeited by virtue of a disqualification order made in respect of the offence of selling or delivering liquor to a person under eighteen;

(4) a justices' licence for any premises is forfeited by virtue of a disqualification order made under s 100 of the LA64 (which lays down the offences for which the court may disqualify persons or premises for Part IV licences);

(5) the holder of a justices' licence for any premises becomes disqualified for the first time for holding such a licence by reason of a conviction for forging a justices' licence or making use of a forged licence knowing it to be forged, or permitting the licensed premises to be a brothel.

The owner or any person on his behalf may apply for a protection order pending a transfer as above provided, notwithstanding the forfeiture.

Note

Not more than one protection order may be granted under these provisions on any forfeiture or disqualification. But where a person is granted a protection order under them the licence may be transferred to him at the first or second licensing sessions begun after the making of the order but not at later sessions.

12 Removals

A removal is the transfer of a licence from one set of premises to another. Removals are of two kinds, special and ordinary.

(a) Special removals (LA64, s 15)

These are granted on the ground either:
(1) that the premises for which the licence was granted are, or are about to be, pulled down or occupied under any Act for the improvement of highways or for any other public purpose; or
(2) that the premises for which the licence was granted have been rendered unfit for use by the business carried on there under the licence by fire, tempest or other unforeseen and unavoidable calamity.

Note

Special removals are only applicable in the case of 'old on-licences'. A special removal cannot be granted to premises in a different licensing district.

(b) Ordinary removals (LA64, s 5)

An ordinary removal is the removal of a licence from one set of premises to another on any ground other than that of a special removal.

The justices may grant an ordinary removal to any premises in their licensing district from any premises whether the old premises are in their district or not. It follows that where a change of district is concerned application for the removal must be made to the licensing justices for the 'receiving' district. A removal may be granted to a person other than the holder of the licence removed. See **3** above for the procedure on a removal. A removal of a justices' on-licence will not be granted unless the premises are suitably adapted.

A removal may be granted before the coming into force of the licence removed or after it has ceased for any reason to be in force.

The justices must not grant the removal unless they are satisfied that no objection to it is made:

(1) in the case of an on-licence by the owner of the premises from which it is sought to remove the licence, or the holder of the licence;

(2) in the case of an off-licence by the holder of the licence; or by any person other than the owner of premises and the holder of the licence or, as the case may be, other than the holder of the licence, whom the justices consider to have a right to object to the removal.

A provisional grant of authority for an ordinary removal may be applied for in respect of an on-licence only, in the same way as the provisional grant of a new on-licence may be applied for.

As to the effect, pending appeal, of a licence granted by way of removal in opposed cases, see LA64, s 27, and **5** above.

No licence can be granted by way of removal of a Part IV licence (see Chapter 2).

For procedure, see Sched 2 of the LA64.

13 Forfeiture of licence

If a licence is forfeited under the provisions mentioned below, the owner of the premises, assuming he is not the licence holder, may usually apply to the appropriate court for a protection order, and if it is granted may carry on business until the first or second sessions after the order is made, when he can apply for a transfer (see **10** above).

(a) Automatic forfeiture

A justices' licence is automatically forfeited in the following cases:

(1) If the licence holder is convicted of making an internal communication between his licensed premises and any unlicensed premises used for public resort or as a refreshment house (LA64, s 184).

(2) If the licence holder is convicted of permitting his licensed premises to be used as a brothel (LA64, s 176).

(3) If the licence holder is convicted for a second time of selling or exposing for sale by retail any intoxicating liquor without a justices' licence, or at a place where he is not authorised by his licence to sell it (LA64, s 160(4)).

(4) In the case of a Part IV licence, if a disqualification order (see Chapter 2) is made (LA64, s 100).

No special order of the court as to forfeiture is required in these cases.

(b) Forfeiture by order of court

A justices' licence may be forfeited by order of the court in the following cases:

(1) If the licence holder is found guilty of permitting a seditious meeting to be held on his premises (Seditious Meetings Act 1817, s 29).

(2) If an alteration is made to any on-licensed premises which:

(*a*) gives increased facilities for drinking in a public or common part of the premises; or

(*b*) conceals from observation a public or common part used for drinking; or

(*c*) affects the communication between the public part where intoxicating liquor is sold and the remainder of the premises or any street or other public way;

without the consent of the licensing justices or as required by some lawful authority (LA64, s 20(3)).

(3) If the licence holder is convicted for a second or subsequent time of an offence under s 169 of the LA64, dealing with the sale etc of intoxicating liquor to persons under eighteen.

14 Revocation

Under LA64, s 20A as inserted by LA88, s 12, licensing justices now have a power to revoke a justices' licence. They can do so at any licensing sessions, other than one at which an application for renewal of the licence falls to be considered, either of their own motion or on the application of any person. This new power is one of great importance. In practice it is most likely to arise from allegations by the police of misconduct or following on complaints from local residents relating to noise or other disturbance. Justices will frequently defer consideration of applications for revocation to a special date in view of their importance and in order to allow time for a full consideration of all the circumstances. The decision to revoke can be made on any ground on which renewal might be refused.

The justices can only exercise the power to revoke if, at least twenty-one days before the commencement of the relevant licensing sessions, notice in writing of the proposal to exercise the power or to make the application has been given to the licence holder and, in the case of an application, to the clerk to the licensing justices which specifies in general terms the grounds on which it is proposed the licence should be revoked. Evidence in revocation proceedings must be given on oath. A decision to revoke has no effect until the time for appealing has expired or until the appeal is disposed of.

15 Licences in suspense (LA64, ss 141–147)

(a) In cases of compulsory acquisition

If the Commissioners of Customs and Excise are satisfied:
(1) that a business is temporarily discontinued by reason of the actual or proposed compulsory acquisition of the licensed premises in which it is carried on; and
(2) that the removal of the licence to other permanent premises reasonably satisfactory to the person by whom the business is carried on is prevented by its being impracticable to provide other such premises;

they shall, on application, grant a certificate to this effect. This certificate puts the justices' licence granted for the premises in suspense. While in suspense it can be transferred (see **10** above) or removed (see **12** above), but it is otherwise not in force for any purpose.

If a licence in suspense is removed (see **12**), it is restored to full force. It may also be so restored if it is proposed to resume on the same site the business formerly carried on at the premises. The holder must then apply to the licensing justices for the district where the premises are situated for their approval of his fitness to hold the licence. If they give this approval and the holder serves notice on their clerk of his proposal to resume the business, the licence is restored to force for all purposes from the time of the giving of the notice. Notice of such a proposal is, however, of no effect unless plans of such works as are reasonably necessary to secure the proper conduct of the business have been submitted to and approved by the justices and the justices have signified their satisfaction that the work has been done.

(b) Other cases of suspension

There are also provisions for the suspension of licences:
(1) where a business has been carried on in temporary premises which cease to be available, and removal of the licence to other premises is impracticable; or
(2) where a business has been discontinued owing to 'war circumstances'.
(LA64, ss 132,141)

(c) Extinguishment of licences in suspense

There are provisions for the extinguishment of licences in suspense when suspension is no longer justified (LA64, s 143). Moreover the Licences in Suspense (Extinguishment) Order 1982 (SI No 1837) states that the removal of licences is not in general prevented in the circumstances referred to above, and that there are now in general no 'war circumstances' justifying suspension. Accordingly licences in suspense due to war circumstances were extinguished (unless again in full force) at the end of one year from the coming into operation of the order on 1 January 1983. Licences otherwise in suspense (unless again in full force) are to be extinguished at the end of five years from that date.

16 Control over the structure of licensed premises (LA64, ss 19,20)

This is exercised by the licensing justices in two principal ways:
(1) No alteration may be made to on-licensed premises if the alteration:
   (*a*) gives increased facilities for drinking in a public or common part of the premises; or
   (*b*) conceals from observation a public or common part used for drinking; or
   (*c*) affects the communication between the public part where intoxicating liquor is sold and the remainder of the premises or any street or other public way;
unless the licensing justices have consented to the alteration or the alteration is required by order of some lawful authority (eg where the local council has ordered sanitary conveniences to be provided).

Before considering an application for consent to alterations the justices may, and usually do, require plans of the proposed alterations to be deposited with their clerk. *Note*   Section 20 does not empower justices to give retrospective consent: *R v Crown Court at Croydon, ex parte Bromley Licensing Justices* (1988) *The Times*, 29 February; 152 JP 245.

Some courts require the service of notices giving details of the application and in particular indicating, if it is the case, how much the licensed area will be increased. Justices often require notices to be served not only on their clerk but also on the police, the local authority and the appropriate fire authority. Some courts take the view that where the increase in the licensed area is substantial then an application should be made for a new licence rather than an application under s 20.

Appeal lies to the Crown Court against refusal of consent.

If such alterations are made without consent, the licence may be declared forfeited or an order may be made that within a fixed time the premises are to be restored to their original condition.

Note

    (*a*) 'Public part' means a part open to customers who are not residents or guests of residents; and 'common part' means a part open generally to all residents or to a particular class of them.

    (*b*) Alterations to off-licensed premises do not require consent. But alterations made to such premises without the justices' approval *may* give ground for a refusal to renew the licence. Accordingly, it is prudent to notify the clerk to the justices of proposed alterations to off-licensed premises.

    (*c*) 'Alterations' may include additions, and the justices, therefore, have power to allow the extension of licensed premises, as well as their rearrangement. But if the premises when altered will have lost their identity, or will no longer be within the ambit of the licence, an application for consent to alterations is inappropriate and a new licence must be applied for.

(2) On any application for the renewal of an on-licence, the justices may require a plan of the premises to be produced before them and to be deposited with their clerk. On renewing the licence, they may order that within a time fixed by the order such structural alterations shall be made to the part of the premises where intoxicating liquor is sold or consumed as they think reasonably necessary to secure the proper conduct of the business (LA64, s 19). They have similar powers in relation to a transfer of a licence whereby its duration is extended (LA64, s 19(6)).

Appeal lies to the Crown Court against such an order.

The clerk to the justices is required to give notice of the making of any such order to the owner of the premises. If any such order is made and complied with, no further requisition for the structural alteration of the premises may be made within the next five years.

17 Occasional licences (LA64, s 180; Finance Act 1967, Sched 7, para 15)

An occasional licence authorises the holder of an on-licence to sell the intoxicating liquor which his licence empowers him to sell at some place other than his ordinary licensed premises, eg at a flower show, or ball or race meeting. In the case of association football matches, see s 5B of the Sporting Events (Control of Alcohol etc) Act 1985. It is granted by the petty sessional court of the district in which the place to which the application relates is situated (not by the licensing justices). It cannot be granted to the holder of a Part IV licence (see Chapter 2) unless the applicant holds a restaurant licence or a residential and restaurant licence and the justices are satisfied that the sale of intoxicating liquor under the occasional licence is to be ancillary to the provision of substantial refreshment.

An occasional licence may not extend over more than three consecutive weeks, nor will it permit sales on Christmas Day, Good Friday or a day of public fast or thanksgiving, but Sundays are not excluded (except in Wales to the extent that Sunday closing remains operative there).

(a) Procedure

The applicant must serve on the chief officer of police (see **3** above) at least twenty-four hours' notice of his intention to apply to the petty sessional court. The notice must state the name and address of the applicant, the place and occasion for which the occasional licence is required, the period for which the applicant desires it to be in force, and the hours to be specified in the licence. The notice may be served personally or sent by post.

The justices may, if they see fit, grant the licence without a hearing if written application is made by lodging two copies of the application with the clerk to the justices not less than one month before the day or earliest day for which application is made. The application must give the particulars required to be given in the notice referred to above.

On receipt of the written application the clerk must serve notice on the chief officer of police by sending him a copy of the application. If not later than seven days after the sending of the notice the police give written notice of objection to the clerk by lodging two copies of the notice with him, the application cannot be granted without a hearing. The hearing can still be dispensed with, however, if the police withdraw their objection by a further notice given in the same way. On receiving a notice of objection or of withdrawal from the police the clerk must send a copy to the applicant.

Where a written application is made to the justices but the application is not granted without a hearing the application may be heard without the applicant having served notice on the police.

18 Occasional permissions

The Licensing (Occasional Permissions) Act 1983 was introduced to enable small organisations to sell liquor at functions connected with their activities. Under it, licensing justices may, if satisfied of certain matters, grant to an officer of an 'eligible organisation' (see below) or of a branch of such organisation an 'occasional permission', allowing him to sell liquor during a period not exceeding twenty-four hours at a function held by the organisation or branch in connection with the organisation's activities.

The justices must be satisfied:

(1) that the officer is a fit and proper person to sell liquor and is resident in their licensing district;

(2) that the place where the function is to be held will be a suitable place for liquor to be sold, and is situated in that district; and

(3) that the sale of liquor at the function is not likely to result in disturbance or annoyance being caused to residents in the neighbourhood of that place, or in any disorderly conduct.

Objectors may be heard.

The justices may attach such conditions to the permission as they think proper. Not more than four permissions may be granted in a licensing district in any period of twelve months in respect of functions held by the same organisation or branch.

An 'eligible organisation' is one not carried on for purposes of private gain. Except in the case of a commercial undertaking a purpose that is calculated to benefit an organisation as a whole is not to be taken to be a purpose of private gain by reason only that action in fulfilment of the purpose would result in benefit to any person as an individual.

(a) Applications for occasional permissions

(1) Applications must be in writing and contain:

(*a*) the name, address and date of birth of the applicant;

(*b*) the name of the organisation in connection with whose activities the function is to be held, the purposes for which the organisation is carried on and (when appropriate) the name of the branch holding the function;

(*c*) the nature of the applicant's office in the organisation or branch holding the function;

(*d*) the date and nature of the function, and the place where it is to be held;

(*e*) the kind or kinds of liquor proposed to be sold at the function and the hours between which it is to be sold;

  (f) details of any occasional permissions granted by the licensing justices in the twelve months preceding the date of the application in respect of functions held by the organisation or branch holding the function.

(2) Two copies of the application must be served on the clerk to the licensing justices not less than one month (ie a calendar month) before the date of the function.

(3) The clerk then must send a copy of the application to the chief officer of police.

(4) The application is heard at the next licensing sessions following its receipt by the clerk; or where those sessions are to be held fifteen days or less after its receipt, at the next following licensing sessions.

(5) The clerk must send the applicant notice of the date, time and place of the sessions at which his application is to be heard.

(6) The applicant must attend the sessions in person if required to do so by the licensing justices, and the justices may postpone consideration of the application until the applicant does attend.

19 Music and dancing

The law relating to the licensing of music and dancing differs according to the location of the premises concerned. Generally speaking, however, notices of application have to be served using the council's own special forms and there are provisions requiring a public display of the notice on the premises and advertising in a local newspaper. Councils also publish a range of fees payable.

(a) Music and dancing in the Greater London Area

Here the licensing authority is the relevant London Borough Council. Under the London Government Act 1963, Sched 12, no premises in Greater London may be used for public dancing, music or other public entertainment of the like kind without a licence from the council. Such a licence remains in force for such a period as the council may determine, which may not be longer than a year, subject to renewal from time to time. There are provisions for the transfer of a licence and for the grant of 'occasional' music licences for one or more specific occasions. Details of the procedure for applications may be obtained from the relevant council's licensing department. There is a right of appeal from the council's decision to the magistrates' court, and thence to the Crown Court.

(b) Music and dancing outside the Greater London Area

Here the licensing authority is the district council for the area to
which licensing functions are assigned by the Local Government
(Miscellaneous Provisions) Act 1982. The Act provides, in general,
that no public music or dancing may be provided in any place except
under the authority of a licence granted by the district council. Such a
licence remains in force for such a period as the district council may
determine, which is not to be longer than one year.

There are provisions for transfer and for the grant of a licence for
one or more particular occasions. The procedure for applications is
set out in Sched 1 to the 1982 Act. Here too there is a right of appeal to
the magistrates' court, and thence to the Crown Court.

(c) Music and dancing in private places of entertainment

Music and dancing or any similar entertainment which is not
'public', and which is promoted for private gain, is controlled by the
Private Places of Entertainment (Licensing) Act 1967. However, this
Act applies only in areas where it has been adopted by the local
authority. Enquiry should be made of the relevant authority as to
procedure, which is not laid down in the Act.

*(d) Public entertainment by radio, TV, recorded sound or live
performers*

By virtue of LA64 s 182, a licence for music and dancing is not
required for premises holding a justices' licence where the public
entertainment is by radio or television or by public entertainment by
way of music and singing only provided solely by recorded sound or
by not more than two performers or sometimes in one of those ways
and sometimes in the other. If both recorded sound and live
performers are providing entertainment at the same time then it seems
that s 182 does not apply and that therefore a music and dancing
licence would be necessary. By way of illustration it would seem that
Karaoke requires an entertainment licence.

20 Performing right licences

(a) Copyright music

The public performance of copyright music is an infringement of
copyright, in respect of which an action may be brought by the owner
of the copyright. A performance of music which can be heard by

customers in, for example, the bar of a public-house is a public performance.

Copyright music may be publicly performed on gramophone records, by means of radio or television broadcasts or by performance in person.

Such performances of copyright music require to be licensed by the owner of the copyright. The Performing Right Society Ltd grants such licences on behalf of most copyright owners, and applications for licences should be addressed to the society at 29 Berners Street, London W1P 4AA.

Note

Although the performance of copyright music at a radio or television studio may have been authorised by the copyright owner, the relaying of such performance over radio or television set counts as a separate performance. Thus a separate licence is required to cover each such public performance.

(b) Gramophone records

There is a separate copyright in gramophone records. Accordingly a licence is needed for the public performance of copyright music on records. This licence is obtained in most cases from Phonographic Performance Ltd, Ganton House, 14–22 Ganton Street, London W1V 1LB.

Note

Such licences are needed to authorise eg the playing of copyright music on gramophone records and tapes in hotel lounges and bars.

21 Permits under GA68 s 34

Premises holding a justices' on-licence may apply to the licensing justices for a permit enabling amusement machines with small prizes to be provided on the premises. In the case of premises holding a Part IV licence the jurisdiction is exercised by the local authority.

The charge for playing a game must not exceed 20p and there are strict limits as to prizes.

The fee at present chargeable for the grant of a permit is £25.00 and in addition there is gaming machine licence duty payable. The authority granting permits has power to limit the number of machines.

22 Appeals to the Crown Court (LA64, ss 21–25)

In the following instances a person aggrieved has a right of appeal under LA64, s 21:

(1) a decision granting a new justices' licence;

(2) a decision refusing a new justices' licence;

(3) a decision granting an ordinary removal of a justices' licence;

(4) a decision refusing an ordinary removal of a justices' licence;

(5) a decision refusing the renewal of a justices' licence;

(6) a decision refusing the transfer of a justices' licence;

(7) a decision refusing the special removal of a justices' licence;

(8) a refusal to declare a provisional grant final;

(9) a refusal to affirm a provisional grant;

(10) a refusal to give consent on the application of the holder of a provisional licence to a modification of plans;

(11) the making of an order to require structural alterations on the renewal of an on-licence;

(12) the refusal of a consent for alterations to on-licensed premises where such consent is required under LA64, s 20;

(13) the revocation of a justices' licence;

(14) any decision as to the conditions of a justices' on-licence.

No person, however, may appeal to the Crown Court against the grant of a justices' licence who has not appeared before the justices and opposed the grant, and no person may appeal against a refusal to attach conditions to a licence or to vary or revoke any previously attached except the person (if any) whose application or request is required for the justices to have jurisdiction to attach or to vary or to revoke conditions. However, where conditions are attached on the applicant's request on the occasion of a renewal, transfer or removal so as to make the licence one of the 'Part IV licences' (see Chapter 2) the applicant for the renewal, transfer or removal may appeal notwithstanding that it was done at his request. (LA64, s 99(4))

On an appeal against the grant of a justices' licence, the applicant for the licence and not the justices must be the respondent, and notice of appeal must be given to him as well as to the clerk of the licensing justices. On an appeal against a refusal to grant a justices' licence or against a decision as to the conditions of a licence, any person who opposed the grant must be a respondent as well as the licensing justices. On an appeal against a decision to revoke a justices' licence any person on whose application the licence was revoked must be a respondent as well as the licensing justices. On an appeal as to the conditions of a licence, or where on appeal the Crown Court grants or confirms the grant of a licence, the court may by its order make any provision as to the attachment of conditions which the justices might have made.

An appeal is by way of a rehearing and therefore the parties are not restricted to the arguments used or evidence advanced at first instance.

(a) Time for appeals

An appeal must be commenced by notice of appeal given to the clerk to the licensing justices within twenty-one days after the decision appealed against. The Crown Court has power to award costs on the determination of an appeal (Crown Court Rules 1982, r 12). A specimen notice of appeal to the Crown Court is shown at Appendix 5. The notice must state the grounds of appeal: see Crown Court Rules 1982.

Chapter 2

Liquor Licensing: Restaurants and Guest Houses; Extensions of Permitted Hours

1 'Part IV licences' (LA64, ss 93–101)

(a) Characteristics

Part IV of the LA64 provides for three specialised types of justices' licence, referred to in the LA64 as 'Part IV licences'. The distinguishing features of these licences are that the justices have only a limited discretion to refuse their grant (see Chapter 1), and there is no requirement to prove 'need', as there generally is in an application for a new licence. The Part IV licences are:

A *The restaurant licence* (LA64, s 94(1))   This covers the sale of liquor with meals. It is defined as a licence which:

(1) is granted for premises structurally adapted and bona fide used or intended to be used for the purpose of providing the customary main meal at midday or in the evening, or both, for the accommodation of persons frequenting the premises; and

(2) is subject to the condition that intoxicating liquor shall not be sold or supplied on the premises otherwise than to persons taking table meals there and for consumption by such a person as an ancillary to his meal.

Note

(1) A table meal is one eaten by a person seated at a table or at a counter or similar structure which serves the purpose of a table and is not used for serving refreshments for consumption by persons not seated at a table or similar structure (LA64, s 201(1)).

(2) The restaurant licence covers the sale or supply of the liquor as an ancillary to a meal. There is no requirement that the liquor is to be served with the meal; and this licence permits, for

example, the service of an aperitif to a customer at (say) a bar, before his meal, as well as the service of a liqueur to a customer in (say) a lounge after his meal.

B *The residential licence* (LA64, s 94(2))   This covers the sale of liquor to residents in residential establishments, eg boarding-houses etc. It is defined as a licence which:

(1) is granted for premises bona fide used or intended to be used for the purpose of habitually providing for reward board and lodging including breakfast and one other at least of the customary main meals; and

(2) is subject to the condition that intoxicating liquor shall not be sold or supplied on the premises other than to persons residing there or their private friends bona fide entertained by them at their own expense, and for consumption by such a person or his private friend so entertained by him either on the premises or with a meal supplied at but to be consumed off the premises.

C *The combined restaurant and residential licence* (LA64, s 94(3)) This covers residential establishments with a public restaurant, and is defined as a licence which:

(1) is granted for premises which come within the descriptions given above for premises qualified to receive a restaurant licence and a residential licence; and

(2) is subject to the condition that liquor shall not be sold or supplied otherwise than as permitted by the conditions of a restaurant licence or by those of a residential licence.

Note

(1) The conditions set out under A(2) above for a restaurant licence (concerning drinks with meals) and those under B(2) for a residential licence (concerning drinks for residents) and any similar conditions attached to a justices' licence:

(*a*) do not extend to the supply of liquor for on-consumption in the exceptional cases where supply out of the permitted hours is allowed by the LA64, ss 59 and 63; and

(*b*) do not extend to sale or supply of liquor under an occasional licence.

(2) A justices' licence does not count as a Part IV licence if it is subject to any condition not required to be attached to it as shown above, unless the condition is one making it a six-day or an early-closing licence (see Chapter 1). But a Part IV licence may be a seasonal licence (see Chapter 1).

(3) It is an implied condition of a Part IV licence that suitable beverages other than intoxicating liquor, including drinking water, shall be equally available for consumption with or otherwise as an ancillary to meals served in the licensed premises (LA64, s 94(5)).

(4) When the justices grant a new residential licence or a new residential and restaurant licence they are bound to attach (unless they consider in the circumstances of the case there is good reason not to do so) a condition that there shall be afforded on the premises for persons paying for board and lodging adequate sitting accommodation in a room not used for sleeping, for serving meals or for the supply and consumption of liquor. Where this condition is not attached on a grant it must be attached on a renewal or transfer if the justices think it required (LA64, s 96).

(b) Grant

Part IV licences can be granted at transfer sessions as well as at Brewster Sessions. The justices can only refuse the grant or renewal or transfer of such a licence on the following grounds (LA64, s 98):

(1) that the applicant is not of full age or is in any other respect not a fit and proper person to hold the licence;

(2) that the premises do not fulfil the requirements laid down for premises for which a Part IV licence is sought (see sub-paras A(1), B(1) and C(1) above), or are not suitable and convenient for the use contemplated having regard to their character and condition, to the nature and extent of the proposed use, and (where it applies) to the required condition as to sitting accommodation, or as to the supply of liquor only as ancillary to a table meal;

(3) that within the twelve months preceding the application:
  (a) a justices' on-licence for the premises has been forfeited (see Chapter 1); or
  (b) the premises have been ill-conducted while a justices' on-licence or a licence under the Late Night Refreshment Houses Act 1969 was in force for them (the Late Night Refreshment Houses Act 1969 provides for the licensing by the local authority of refreshment houses which do not supply liquor, but are open after 10 pm, eg all-night cafés); or
  (c) the required condition as to sitting accommodation has been habitually broken while a residential licence or a

residential and restaurant licence (or other licence with the like condition) was in force for the premises; or

(*d*) the condition as to the availability of beverages other than intoxicating liquor has been habitually broken while a special licence or other licence with a like condition was in force for the premises;

(4) in the case of a restaurant or restaurant and residential licence, that the trade done in the premises in providing refreshment to persons resorting there (but not provided with board and lodging) does not habitually consist to a substantial extent of providing table meals of a kind to which the consumption of liquor might be ancillary;

(5) that the sale or supply of liquor on the premises is undesirable;

(*a*) in the case either of a residential licence or residential and restaurant licence, because a large proportion of the persons provided with board and lodging is habitually made up of young persons unaccompanied (this phrase means persons under eighteen not accompanied and paid for by a parent or a person of full age); or

(*b*) in the case either of a restaurant licence or a residential and restaurant licence, because a large proportion of the persons resorting to the premises but not provided with board and lodging is habitually made up of young persons unaccompanied; or

(*c*) in the case of any Part IV licence, because the contemplated service of liquor would be by self-service methods—ie any method allowing a customer to help himself on payment or before payment;

(6) if it appears to the justices on an application for the grant or renewal of a Part IV licence that the local authority, the fire authority or the police desired to inspect the premises, and took reasonable steps to do so, but were unable to carry out an inspection.

Where the justices refuse an application for the grant or renewal of any on-licence other than a Part IV licence, they must at the applicant's request treat him as having made an alternative application for a Part IV licence for the sale of such descriptions of liquor as he may specify in his request (LA64, s 99(1)).

On the renewal, transfer or removal of any on-licence the applicant may, with the consent of the registered owner (if any) of the premises, request that the licence be varied by attaching conditions making it a Part IV licence. If the justices make such variation, the renewal, transfer or removal must not be refused except on the grounds on which a renewal of the relevant type of licence may be refused.

Where the justices refuse an application for the grant or renewal of a Part IV licence they must specify in writing to the applicant the grounds of refusal.

No licence may be granted by way of the removal of a Part IV licence (LA64, s 93(4)).

(c) Disqualification for Part IV licences (LA64, ss 100, 101)

Where a person is convicted of any of certain specified offences he may be disqualified from holding such a licence or a licence under the Late Night Refreshment Houses Act 1969, and the court may also disqualify the premises.

A disqualification order may at the discretion of the court be either:

(1) an order disqualifying the person convicted for such period as may be specified in the order (but not exceeding five years from the date the order comes into force) from holding or obtaining licences of the relevant types; or

(2) an order prohibiting licences of the relevant types from being held or granted within such period as aforesaid, by or to any person in respect of the premises at which the offence in question was committed; or

(3) an order incorporating both such a disqualification and such a prohibition.

If one of these orders is made, any licence within the disqualification or prohibition, if previously obtained, will be forfeited or if subsequently obtained will be null and void.

A court must not make a disqualification order containing a prohibition on the holding or grant of licences in respect of premises specified in the order unless an opportunity has been given to any person interested in the premises (eg the freeholder) and applying to be heard by the court to show cause why the order should not be made.

(1) *Suspension of disqualification pending appeal*   The justices may, on such conditions as they think just, suspend the operation of a disqualification order, with a view to enabling a licence to remain in force pending an appeal against the conviction or against the making of the order, or pending the consideration of an appeal; unless an order is so suspended it comes into force the day it is made.

(2) *Revocation of disqualification*   At any time while a disqualification order is in force a magistrates' court on complaint made by

any person affected by the order may revoke the order or vary it by reducing any period of disqualification or prohibition specified in the order; and any person who has made such a complaint may, if aggrieved by the court's decision, appeal to the Crown Court. Where a complaint is made to revoke or vary a disqualification order the summons granted on the complaint must be served on the chief officer of police for the area where the premises are situated.

(3) *Offences for which disqualification orders may be made*   These offences are specified in LA64, s 100(4), and include selling liquor in breach of the licensing conditions, permitting drunkenness, permitting unlawful gaming, and allowing prostitutes to assemble on the premises.

These powers are in addition to the court's existing powers to disqualify and forfeit licences (see Chapter 1).

Where a Part IV licence is forfeited by a disqualification order, the court may grant a protection order (see Chapter 1) to any owner of the premises or to any other person authorised by an owner of the premises and the licence may subsequently be transferred to that person (LA64, s 10(3)(*d*)).

(d) Notices

The holder of a residential licence is not required to display a notice on the premises showing that he is licensed to sell liquor. The holder of a restaurant or restaurant and residential licence must display a notice, but the notice need only state his name, the word 'licensed', and words to express that he is licensed to sell liquor for consumption on the premises with meals (LA64, s 183(2)).

2 Orders of exemption ('extensions') (LA64, ss 74,75)

Orders of exemption may be granted to allow on-licence holders and the secretaries of registered clubs (see Chapter 3) to sell and supply liquor outside the ordinary permitted hours.

These orders are often popularly referred to as 'extensions'.

(a) Procedure

Application should be made to the appropriate clerk to the magistrates or police authority for details of the procedure for obtaining orders of exemption. This procedure varies slightly in different areas. Orders of exemption are not licences.

Orders of exemption are of two kinds—general and special.

(b) General orders of exemption

Petty sessions has power to grant an order of exemption adding specified hours to the ordinary permitted hours where application is made to it by the holder of a justices' licence or the secretary of a registered club situated in the immediate neighbourhood of a public market or of a place where persons follow a lawful trade or calling.

The court must be satisfied that the order asked for is desirable for the accommodation of any considerable number of persons attending the market or following the trade in question. The court may at any time revoke or vary the order.

Note

General orders of exemption are usually more or less permanent in form, being intended to meet a more or less permanent need felt by some particular class of persons, eg workers at 'all-night' flower or vegetable markets. As to the duty of the licence holder to display a notice stating the effect of the order, see LA64, s 89.

(c) Special orders of exemption

The authority for the grant of these orders consists of:
(1) In the City of London, the Commissioner of Police for the City of London.
(2) In the Metropolitan Police District, the Commissioner of Police.
(3) Elsewhere, petty sessions.

The authority has power to grant a special order of exemption adding specified hours to the ordinary permitted hours when application is made by the holder of a justices' licence or the secretary of a registered club in connection with a special occasion (eg a ball or dinner at which it is desired to serve drinks up to a later hour than usual). The permitted hours on such a special occasion may be extended to any time which the authority thinks fit. The authority has a discretion as to what constitutes a 'special occasion'. This has been given extensive judicial consideration. The courts have laid down three criteria:
(1) Is the occasion one which in law is capable of being a special occasion?
(2) If it is, then do the justices have material available to show that the occasion is special in the locality in which the premises are situated?
(3) Is the occasion so frequent as not to be special?

As in the case of the grant of occasional licences the special order of exemption may be granted by justices outside London without a hearing if a written application is made by lodging two copies of the application with the clerk to the justices not less than one month before the day or earliest day for which application is made. The same rules apply about police objections.

Note

The occasional licence and the special order of exemption should not be confused. The former authorises the supply of liquor at a different place from the usual one and the latter at a different time.

3 'Restaurant' or 'supper hours' certificates (LA64, ss 68,69)

The holder of a justices' on-licence or the secretary of a registered club at whose premises there is accommodation for and a habitual service (actual or intended) of meals may apply to the justices for this certificate, the grant of which adds on Sundays, Christmas Day and Good Friday the period between the first and second parts of the general licensing hours, and an extra hour in the evenings to the general licensing hours for the purpose of the sale or supply to persons taking table meals of intoxicating liquor supplied in a part of the premises usually set apart for the service of such persons, and supplied for consumption as an ancillary to a meal. For any other purpose, or in any other part of the premises, the permitted hours remain unaffected by the certificate. Such certificates are still sometimes called 'supper hours' certificates', since their original purpose was to add an extra hour for the service of drinks in the evening. Their effect is to certify that the justices are satisfied of the two specific matters mentioned in the next paragraph.

Before they grant a certificate, the justices must be satisfied that the premises are structurally adapted, and bona fide used or intended to be used for the purpose of habitually providing for the accommo- dation of persons frequenting the premises substantial refreshment, to which the sale and supply of intoxicating liquor is ancillary. 'Substantial refreshment' means table meals (ie meals eaten by a person seated at a table, or at a counter or other structure serving the purpose of a table, which is not used for the service of refreshments for consumption by persons not seated at a table or structure serving the purpose of a table) (LA64, ss 68(3) and 201). The question of what constitutes a 'meal' is one of fact for the justices.

(a) Application: licensed premises

The procedure for application for a certificate is laid down in the Licensing Rules 1961 (SI No 2477). Seven days at least (ie eight days) before the sessions at which the application will be made the applicant must send to the chief officer of police (see Chapter 1), and to the clerk to the licensing justices, notice of his intention to apply. The notice may be sent by post. The notice must be signed by the applicant or his authorised agent, and state the address of the relevant premises. The notice to the police may specify the date (not being less than fourteen days later) on which, if the certificate is granted, the applicant intends to make use of it to extend the hours. Otherwise, by s 69 of the LA64, the licence holder must give a separate notice to the chief officer of police of the day when he will apply the extended hours to his premises. Such notice must be served not less than fourteen days before the day in question.

A specimen form of notice of application for a certificate in respect of licensed premises is shown at Appendix 3.

(b) Application: registered club

By s 92 of the LA64, the procedure for application in the case of a registered club is in accordance with the provision of Sched 6 to the Act, relating to applications for registration certificates, subject to any necessary modifications. This procedure is outlined in Chapter 3.

(c) Withdrawal and abandonment of certificate

The certificate remains in force until withdrawn. If any question arises as to its withdrawal, notice in writing may be served on its holder not less than seven days before the commencement of the annual licensing meeting. The justices then consider whether the certificate is to be withdrawn, and the procedure is the same as where there is opposition to the renewal of a licence.

Where the licence holder or club secretary intends to abandon the extension, he must give notice to the chief officer of police not less than fourteen days before 4 April in any year (ie the notice must be served not later than 20 March in the year concerned). The extension then terminates on 4 April.

As to the duty of a licence-holder to display on the licensed premises a notice stating the effect of s 68, see LA64, s 89.

4 'Special hours' certificates (LA64, ss 76–83)

A 'special hours' certificate may be applied for in respect of premises, such as late-night restaurants, where music and dancing take place and meals are served. The effect of the certificate is generally to extend the permitted hours until 2 am (3 am in parts of London) if music and dancing continue until that time. 'Drinking up' time is thirty minutes. See below as to the court's power to limit the extended hours. Such certificates may be obtained for licensed premises and for registered clubs. The granting authority is the licensing justices in the case of licensed premises, and the magistrates' court in the case of registered clubs. The authority must be satisfied (in the case of licensed premises) that a music and dancing licence is in force for the premises and that the whole or any part of the premises is structurally adapted and bona fide used or intended to be used for the purpose of providing for persons resorting to the premises music and dancing and substantial refreshment to which the sale of liquor is ancillary. In the case of registered clubs, the authority must be satisfied that a special certificate from the licensing authority for music and dancing as to the suitability of the premises is in force, and as above, in relation to the adaptation and actual or intended use of the premises. If satisfied on these matters the authority (ie the licensing justices or magistrates court) may grant the certificate with or without limitations. The Licensing Act 1988, s 5(1) makes it clear that the justices are no longer under a duty to grant the certificate even if so satisfied.

Note

(1) A special hours certificate may not be limited in duration (ie it remains in force until revoked under s 81), and does not require renewal.

(2) 'Providing' music and dancing and refreshment means providing them on every weekday or on particular weekdays in any week, subject to any break for a period or periods not exceeding two weeks in any twelve successive months, or on any special occasion or by reason of any emergency. Providing facilities for dancing means providing facilities that are adequate having regard to the number of persons for whose reception on the premises provision is made (LA64, s 83).

(3) Where a special hours certificate is granted for premises which are used or intended to be used only on particular weekdays for the provision of music and dancing and refreshment, the certificate must be limited to those days in the week on which it is shown that music and dancing and refreshment are or are intended to be provided (LA64, s 80(1)).

(4) A club holding a justices' licence must obtain a certificate of

suitability of the club premises for music and dancing before it can obtain a special hours certificate.

(5) The certificate takes effect from such day as the licensee or the secretary of the club fixes by notice in writing to the chief officer of police, served not less than fourteen clear days before such day. Such notice may be included in the notice given of the application (see below).

(6) When granting a special hours certificate the justices are entitled, under the new provisions of LA64, s 78A (as inserted by LA88, s 5(2)), to attach limitations to the certificate whether granted with respect to licensed premises or a club. The power to do so is distinct from the duty to do so under LA64, s 80. The limitations may only relate to particular times of the day, particular days of the week or particular periods of the year. Once made the limitations can be varied on the application of the licensee or club. In addition, under s 81A (as substituted by LA88, s 5(4)) the justices have further powers to impose limitations as to hours. These powers may be exercised on an application to revoke the special hours certificate or in respect of premises outside certain areas of London, on the application of the chief officer of police. The procedure in the case of applications under s 81A(2) or (3) is to be found in the Licensing (Special Hours Certificates) Rules 1982 (SI No 1384) as amended by the Licensing (Special Hours Certificates) (Amendment) Rules 1988 (SI No 1338). Any such limitation may be varied on the application of the licensee or club.

(7) A special hours certificate may be revoked in certain circumstances; eg the police may apply for revocation on the ground of disorderly conduct on the premises (see s 81 of the LA64).

(8) The Licensing Act 1964, s 81B makes provision for appeals where the justices have:

(a) not granted a special hours certificate,

(b) revoked or not revoked a special hours certificate,

(c) attached or not attached limitations under s 78A or s 81A.

The appellant can be 'any person aggrieved' by the decision, except that under the new s 81B(2) (as substituted by LA88, Sched 3, para 9), only the chief officer of police may appeal against a decision not to revoke a certificate or not to attach a limitation under s 81A(3). Only if a person has appeared before the justices and made representations that a limitation under s 81A(2) should be attached can he appeal against a decision not to attach such a limitation. A person can only be made a respondent to an appeal if he made representations before the justices.

(9) It is possible to have both an extended hours order and a special hours certificate in respect of the same premises (LA64, s 82(2)).

(a) Application: licensed premises

The procedure for application is laid down in the Licensing (Special Hours Certificates) Rules 1982 (SI No 1384) as amended by the Licensing (Special Hours Certificate) Amendment Rules 1988 (SI No 1338). At least twenty-one days (ie twenty-two days) before applying to the licensing justices the applicant must give notice in writing to the chief officer of police and to the clerk to the licensing justices of his intention to make the application. The notice must be signed by the applicant or his authorised agent, and state the address of the relevant premises. A specimen form of notice of application is shown at Appendix 4.

Not more than twenty-eight days nor less than fourteen days before applying, the applicant must both display a notice of his intention to make the application for a period of seven days on or near the premises so that it can be read by the public and advertise such a notice in a local newspaper.

Not later than seven days before the commencement of the licensing sessions at which the application is to be made, a person intending to oppose an application for the grant of a special hours certificate or for the variation of any limitation under s 78A(4) must give written notice of his intention to the applicant and to the clerk to the justices specifying in general terms the ground of opposition. Failure to comply with these formalities precludes the justices from entertaining the objection.

The Rules also set out procedures relevant to applications for the revocation of a special hours certificate under LA64, s 81(2) or (4) and for applications under LA64, s 81A(3) for the attachment of any limitation to the certificate or for the variation of any such limitation.

(b) Application: registered club

By s 92 of the LA64, the procedure for application in the case of a registered club is in accordance with the provision of Sched 6 to the Act, relating to applications for registration certificates, subject to any necessary modifications. This procedure is outlined in Chapter 3. As noted above, the application in such a case is made to the magistrates' court, not to the licensing justices. The secretary of the club must first obtain a certificate of the suitability of the premises for music and dancing from the relevant authority. This is the authority which has power to grant music and dancing licences in the area. No special procedure is laid down for applying for this certificate of suitability. Enquiry should be made of the clerk to the authority as to the form which the application should take.

Note

(1) When the secretary applies to the relevant authority for their certificate of suitability in respect of the premises, the authority *may* grant it if satisfied that the premises (whether or not they are kept or intended to be kept for dancing, music or other public entertainment of the like kind) in all other respects fulfil the authority's requirements for the grant of a music and dancing licence.

(2) The authority may grant such a certificate on such terms, and subject to such conditions or restrictions, as it thinks fit.

(3) Such a certificate remains in force for such period as may be specified therein.

(4) The authority may, on application by the club secretary, renew it from time to time.

(5) The authority may, on application by the secretary, waive or modify any condition or restriction subject to which it was granted or renewed.

(6) The authority has power to revoke the certificate where a condition or restriction is not complied with; but the club has a right to be heard before this is done (LA64, s 79).

5 Extended hours orders (LA64, ss 70–73)

A further method by which the permitted hours for the sale of liquor may be extended is provided by ss 70–73 of the LA64, which provide for extensions in premises which provide 'live' entertainment. 'Entertainment' does not include forms of entertainment otherwise than by persons actually present and performing. The extension is only available to premises which have a restaurant or 'supper hours' certificate (see **3** above), permitting sale in the hour following the general licensing hours. It also is only available where the premises are structurally adapted and bona fide used or intended to be used for the purpose of habitually providing, for the accommodation of persons frequenting them, musical or other entertainment as well as substantial refreshment (see **3** above); and the sale and supply of liquor is ancillary to that refreshment and entertainment. The extension is to 1 am on weekdays on which the entertainment is provided; and the purpose for which the time is added is (in any part habitually set apart from the provision of the refreshment and entertainment) the sale and supply, before the provision of the entertainment or the provision of substantial refreshment has ended, of liquor for consumption in such part; and the consumption of liquor so supplied. 'Drinking up' time is thirty minutes.

The extension is available to licensed premises and registered clubs. To obtain it, application must be made for an 'extended hours order'.

(a) Application: licensed premises

The procedure for application is laid down in s 71(3) of the LA64 and the Licensing (Extended Hours Orders) Rules 1962 (SI No 75) as amended by the Licensing (Extended Hours Orders) (Amendment) Rules 1988 (SI No 1188). It follows the procedure on the consideration of the grant of a new justices' licence, with any necessary modifications (see Chapter 1) unless the application is for the revocation of such an order, in which case the procedure follows that of the opposition to a renewal. Notice of application must be given to the persons in the manner and at the times required by Sched 2 to the LA64. If by inadvertence or misadventure the applicant fails to give proper notice of the application the justices may postpone consideration of his application subject to such terms as they impose, and may grant it on postponed consideration if the terms were complied with. When an order is made the licensee must within fourteen days give notice of its making to the chief officer of police.

(b) Application: registered club

By s 92 of the LA64 the procedure for application in the case of a registered club is in accordance with the provisions of Sched 6 to the Act, relating to applications for registration certificates, subject to any necessary modifications. This procedure is outlined in Chapter 3. The application in such a case is made to the magistrates' court, not to the licensing justices. When an order is made the secretary of the club must within fourteen days give written notice thereof of its making to the chief officer of police, sending with the notice a copy of the order (LA64, s 72(3)).

Note

The following points should be noted in regard to such orders, whether made in respect of licensed premises or registered clubs.

(1) The order no longer requires annual renewal. It lapses when the licence ceases to be in force otherwise than on its being

superseded on renewal or transfer. It may be varied by a further order.

(2) The making of the order is discretionary.

(3) The order must be revoked if the justices or the magistrates' court are satisfied on an application by the police either:

    (*a*) that use of the premises for the specified purpose (ie for habitually providing music or other entertainment as well as substantial refreshment) has not been made; or

    (*b*) that it is expedient to revoke the order by reason of undesirable conduct in the premises, or by reason of the conduct of persons resorting thereto, or of any actual or likely annoyance resulting from it to occupiers or inmates of nearby premises, or by reason of the ill-conduct of the premises (LA64, s 73(4)).

(4) The order may not be made unless it is shown that the condition above referred to as the actual or intended use of the premises is satisfied in relation to the premises or part thereof, to the periods, to the weekdays and to the times for which the order is to have effect, and that the premises or part are structurally adapted for the specified purpose. But the licensing justices or the magistrates' court may assume when making an order to vary a previous one that the conditions for the making of the previous order are still satisfied (LA64, s 73(1)).

(5) The licensing justices or magistrates' court may refuse to make the order, or limit its operation to part of the premises, or to particular periods of the year, or to particular weekdays, or to a time earlier than 1 am, if it appears reasonable to do so having regard to all the circumstances, and in particular the comfort and convenience of the occupiers and inmates of nearby premises.

(6) The order comes into force as soon as it is made. The licensee or club secretary must give notice of its making, and send a copy of it, to the chief officer of police within fourteen days.

Chapter 3

Clubs

Intoxicating liquor may be served in clubs under the authority of either a registration certificate under Part II of the LA64 or an ordinary justices' licence. Broadly speaking, a registration certificate is the appropriate authority for a members' club, which generally does not require a licence, since if the ownership of the stock of liquor is vested in the members no 'sale' occurs when a member obtains a drink. Proprietary clubs, on the other hand, where the proprietor sells liquor to the members, require to be licensed. Some members' clubs, moreover, which do not wish or are unable to comply with the qualifications of the LA64 as to registration, require to be licensed, even though no 'sale' of liquor occurs on the premises. This is possible under s 55 of the LA64 (see **8** below).

It is generally advantageous for a club to apply for a registration certificate rather than for a licence (if it is qualified so to do), because where a licence is applied for, the justices have an unfettered discretion to refuse the grant. They can only refuse a certificate on certain specified grounds (LA64, s 40(6)).

Where a licence is granted to a club, or a club proprietor, the justices usually impose a condition (under their general power as to conditions, see LA64, s 4) that there shall be no sale to non-members, and frequently that forty-eight hours shall elapse between a member's nomination and admission. These are sometimes called 'club conditions'.

Application must be made for the registration certificate to the magistrates' court (see **2** below). It is only granted or renewed if the qualifications of the Act are satisfied. Provision is made for objections to registration or renewal. One certificate may relate to any number of premises of the same club, and on application the certificate may be varied as regards the premises to which it relates.

A registration certificate granted by a magistrates' court has effect for twelve months. It may, however, be renewed. Where an application for renewal of a certificate is made not less than twenty-eight days before the certificate expires, the certificate continues in force until the application is disposed of by the court or the court otherwise orders. It may also at any time be surrendered by the club. A certificate may not be refused by the magistrates in the absence of a properly made objection except on certain fixed grounds, and the magistrates are required to state in writing the grounds of any refusal to issue or renew a certificate. A second or subsequent renewal may be for a term up to ten years.

1 Qualifications for registration (LA64, s 41)

A   A club is only qualified to have a certificate if under its rules persons may not be admitted to membership, or admitted as candidates to any membership privileges, without an interval of at least two days between their nomination or application for membership and their admission. Persons becoming members without prior nomination or application may not be admitted to membership privileges without an interval of at least two days between their becoming members and their admission.

B   A club is only qualified to have a certificate for any premises if:
  (1) it is established and conducted in good faith as a club, and has not less than twenty-five members; and
  (2) intoxicating liquor is not supplied, or intended to be supplied, to members on the premises otherwise than by or on behalf of the club; and
  (3) the purchase for the club, and the supply by the club of intoxicating liquor (so far as not managed by the club in general meeting or otherwise by the general body of members) is managed by an elective committee as defined in the Act (Sched 7; see Note (2) below).

Note
  (1) In determining whether a club is established and conducted in good faith as a club the magistrates may have regard:
    (*a*) to any arrangement restricting the club's freedom of purchase of intoxicating liquor (ie whether it is 'tied' or not); and
    (*b*) to any provision in the rules, or arrangement, under which money or property of the club, or any gain arising from the

carrying on of the club, is or may be applied otherwise than for the benefit of the club as a whole or for charitable, benevolent or political purposes; and

(c) to the arrangements for giving members proper information as to the finances of the club and to the accounts and other records kept to ensure the accuracy of that information; and

(d) to the nature of the premises occupied by the club.

Where the rules of a club applying for the issue or renewal of a certificate conform with the requirements of Sched 7 to the LA64 (see **7** below) the court must assume as regards any matters not raised by an objection duly made that the club satisfies the qualification requirements set out under B(1), (2) and (3) above and, in the case of a renewal, those set out under C(1) and (2) below.

The court, however, may nevertheless enquire, if it sees fit, whether there is:

(i) any arrangement restricting the club's freedom of purchase of liquor; or

(ii) any provision in the rules or arrangement under which money or property of the club, or any gain arising from the carrying on of the club, is or may be applied otherwise than for the benefit of the club as a whole or for charitable, benevolent or political purposes. If there is any such arrangement or provision the court may enquire whether it is such that the club ought not to be treated as established and conducted in good faith as a club.

(2) An 'elective committee' means a committee consisting of members of the club who are elected to the committee of the club for a term of not less than one year nor more than five years.

Elections to the committee must be held annually, and if all the elected members do not go out of office in every year, there must be fixed rules for determining those that are to do so, and all members of the club entitled to vote at the election and of not less than two years' standing must be equally capable of being elected (subject only to any provision made for nomination of members of the club and to any provision prohibiting or restricting re-election) and if nomination is required must have equal rights to nominate persons for election.

A committee of which not less than two-thirds of the members were elected as above is treated as an elective committee except in the case of a committee with less than four members or of a committee concerned with the purchase for the club or with the supply by the club of liquor. A sub-committee of an elective committee is treated as an elective committee if its members are appointed by the committee and not less than two-thirds of them (or, in the case of a sub-committee having less than four members or concerned with the purchase for the club or the supply by the club of liquor, all of them) are duly elected committee members who go out of office in the sub-committee on ceasing to be members of the committee.

Where the rules of a club make provision for a class of members to have limited rights or no rights of voting in regard to the affairs of the club, then the questions whether the arrangements for the supply of liquor are under the control of an elective committee or whether the rules of the club conform to the requirements of Sched 7 are, if the court so directs, determined as if the exclusion of the particular class from voting to the extent provided for by the rules were authorised by the provisions of the Act as to voting at general meetings or elections; but the court must not so direct unless it is satisfied that the provision made by the rules is part of a genuine arrangement made in the interests of the club as a whole and of that class of members for facilitating the membership of people precluded by distance or other circumstances from making full use of membership privileges, and it is not designed to secure for a minority an unfair measure of control over the club's affairs.

If the club is a registered society within the meaning of the Industrial and Provident Societies Act 1965 or the Friendly Societies Act 1974, the rule that the purchase and supply of liquor must be managed by an elective committee is satisfied so long as the matter is under the control of the members or of a committee appointed by the members. In such a case the rules of the club are treated as if they conformed to the statutory requirements in Sched 7 so long as they conform with those requirements as regards voting at general meetings and as regards election or admission to membership (LA64, s 42). (See **7** below for these requirements.)

C   A club is only qualified to have a certificate for any premises if no arrangements are, or are intended to be made:

(1) for any person to receive at the expense of the club any commission, percentage or similar payment on or with reference to purchases of intoxicating liquor by the club; or

(2) for any person directly or indirectly to derive any pecuniary benefit from the supply of intoxicating liquor by or on behalf of the club to members or guests, apart from any benefit accruing to the club as a whole and apart also from any benefit which a

person derives indirectly by reason of the supply giving rise or contributing to a general gain from the carrying on of the club (LA64, s 41(2)(*d*)).

2 Application for a certificate (LA64, Sched 5)

(1) The application must specify the name, objects and address of the club, and must state that there is kept at the address a list of the names and addresses of members.

(2) The application must state that the club is qualified to receive a registration certificate for the premises. In other words, it must state that it fulfils the qualifications set out in **1** above.

(3) The application must set out, or incorporate a document annexed which sets out, the names and addresses of the members of any committee having the general management of the club's affairs, and those of the members of any other committee concerned with the purchase for the club or supply by the club of liquor, and those of other officers of the club.

(4) The application must state, or incorporate a document annexed which states, the rules of the club or, in the case of an application for renewal, the changes in the rules made since the last application for the grant or renewal of the certificate.

If, in the case of an application for renewal, there has been no change in the rules since the last application, the application must say so.

(5) The application must:
    (*a*) identify the premises concerned; and
    (*b*) state that those premises are or are to be occupied by and habitually used for club purposes, the times at which they are or are to be opened to members and the hours (if any) fixed by or under the rules of the club as the permitted hours there; and
    (*c*) state the interest held by or in trust for the club in those premises and, if it is leasehold interest or if the club has no interest, the name and address of any person to whom payment is or is to be made of rent under the lease or otherwise for the use of the premises.

(6) (*a*) The application must give, or incorporate a document annexed giving:
      (i) particulars of any property not comprised in the particulars of the premises referred to above which is or is to be used for club purposes and not held by or in trust for the club absolutely, including the name and

address of any person to whom payment is or is to be made for use of that property;

(ii) particulars of any liability of the club in respect of principal or interest of moneys borrowed by the club or charged on property held by or in trust for the club, including the name and address of the person to whom payment is or is to be made on account of that principal or interest;

(iii) particulars of any liability of the club, or of a trustee for the club in respect of which any person has given any guarantee or provided any security, together with particulars of the guarantee or security given or provided, including the name and address of the person giving or providing it.

(b) An application for renewal, or document annexed to it, may give the above particulars by reference to the changes (if any) since the last application by the club for the issue or renewal of the certificate.

(c) If there is no property or liability of which particulars are required as above, the application must say so.

(7) (a) The application must give, or must incorporate a document annexed giving particulars of any premises not comprised in the particulars referred to above which have within the last twelve months been occupied and habitually used for club purposes, and must state the interest then held by or in trust for the club in those premises, and if it was a leasehold interest or if the club had no interest, the name and address of any person to whom payment was made of rent under the lease or otherwise for use of the premises.

(b) If there are no such premises the application must say so.

(8) Where the interest held by or in trust for the club in any land of which particulars are required as above is or was a leasehold interest, and the rent under the lease is not or was not paid by the club or the trustees for the club, the application must give the name and address of the person by whom it is or was paid.

For procedure on the application, see **6** below.

3 Refusal of a certificate (LA64, s 43)

The magistrates may refuse an application for the issue or renewal of a certificate if it is proved that a person who is likely during the currency of the certificate to take an active part in the management of the club is not a fit person, in view of his known character as proved to the court, to be concerned in the management of a registered club. A certificate will not be issued or renewed or have effect for premises disqualified for use as a registered club, for licensed premises, nor for premises which include or form part of disqualified or licensed premises.

The magistrates may also refuse an application for the issue or renewal of a certificate:

(1) if the premises or any premises including or forming part of them have been licensed premises within the twelve months before the application but have ceased to be licensed premises by forfeiture of the licence or by the refusal of an application to renew it or because the licence has been revoked; or

(2) if the club has other club premises which are licensed premises and the court is of the opinion that the issue or renewal of the registration certificate is likely to give occasion for abuse by reason of any difference in the permitted hours in the premises or otherwise.

For other grounds for refusal of a certificate, see **4** below.

4 Objections to and cancellations of registration (LA64, s 44)

Objections to an application for the issue or renewal of a certificate can be made on certain specified grounds by the chief officer of police, the local council or any person 'affected by reason of his occupation of or interest in other premises'. The grounds are as follows:

(1) that the application does not give the information required by the Act, or the information is incomplete, or inaccurate, or the application is otherwise not in conformity with the Act (see **2** above for rules concerning the application);

(2) that the premises are not suitable and convenient for the purpose in view of their character and condition and of the size and nature of the club;

(3) that the club does not satisfy the statutory rules for qualification to receive a certificate (see Note (2) to **1** above for these requirements), or that the application must or ought to be refused on the grounds set out in **3** above;

(4) that the club is conducted in a disorderly manner or for an unlawful purpose, or that the rules of the club are habitually disregarded in respect of the admission of persons to member-

ship or to privileges of membership or in any other material respect;

(5) that the club premises (including premises in respect of which the club is not registered or seeking registration) are habitually used for an unlawful purpose, or for indecent displays, or as a resort of criminals or prostitutes, or that in such premises there is frequent drunkenness, or there have been within the preceding twelve months illegal sales of intoxicating liquor, or persons not qualified to get intoxicating liquor there are habitually admitted for the purpose of obtaining it.

For the form of objection, see **6** below.

The court, if satisfied that the ground of objection is made out, may refuse the application and, in the case of an objection on any of the grounds shown under (1) to (3) above, *must* do so. However, in the case of an objection made on ground (2) (that the premises are not suitable and convenient) the court may abstain from refusing the application if it thinks it reasonable not to refuse having regard to any steps taken or proposed to be taken to remove the ground of objection.

Where a club seeks or holds a certificate for two or more premises not contiguous to one another, the court on an objection may refuse to issue or renew it, or may cancel it for part of the premises only, if the ground of objection relates only to that part, or is only proved in relation to that part, and if the court is of the opinion that it is reasonable in the circumstances for the club to be or remain registered in respect of the other part. No order may be made forbidding any premises to be used or occupied for club purposes (as to which see below) unless the ground of objection or complaint relates to and is proved for those premises or adjoining premises (LA64, s 52(3) and (4)).

A complaint for the cancellation of an existing certificate may be made by the chief officer of police or the local authority on any of grounds (3), (4) or (5) above; and the court, if satisfied that on such an objection the application for renewal must or ought to be refused on that ground, must cancel the certificate. As to service of the summons etc, see **6** below.

For procedure on objections, see **6** also.

5 Disqualifying premises (LA64, s 47)

Where a club is registered in respect of any premises and the court cancels or refuses to renew the certificate for those premises on any ground mentioned under (3), (4) or (5) above, the court may order that, for a period specified in the order, the premises shall not be occupied and used for the purpose of any registered club. The period specified, however, may not exceed one year unless the premises have been subject to a previous order of the same kind, or to a similar order under any previous enactment about clubs (eg the Licensing Act 1953) and shall not in any case exceed five years.

At any time while an order of this kind is in force a magistrates' court may revoke or vary it on an application by any person affected. In such a case the summons must be served on the chief officer of police and the local authority.

6 Procedure

(a) On application or surrender

(1) Application for registration must generally be made to the magistrates' court acting for the petty sessions area in which the premises are situated. The application must be heard in open court by not less than two magistrates or by a stipendiary magistrate alone and in general the procedure for the hearing of an ordinary complaint in such a court must be followed.

(2) (a) An application for the issue, renewal or variation of a certificate is made by lodging the application, together with the required number of additional copies (see (e) below) with the magistrates' clerk. For the form of the application, see 2 above.

(b) The court may allow applications to be amended on such conditions as it thinks fit.

(c) A certificate is surrendered by lodging with the clerk a notice of surrender together with the certificate and the required number (see (e) below) of additional copies of the notice.

(d) Any such application, amended application and notice must be signed by the chairman or secretary of the club.

(e) When he receives such an application or notice the magistrates' clerk must at once send a copy to any chief officer of police and to the clerk of any local council concerned. The number of additional copies required to be lodged with the clerk is the number which he needs for these purposes.

(f) A club applying for the issue of a certificate for any premises or for the renewal of a certificate in respect of different, additional or enlarged premises must give public notice of the application (identifying the premises and giving the name and address of the club) either:

(i) by displaying the notice on or near the premises, in a place where it can conveniently be read by the public for seven days beginning with the date of the application; or

(ii) by advertisement on one at least of those days in a newspaper circulating in the place where the premises are situated.

(b) On objections

(1) (a) An objection to an application for the issue or renewal of a certificate must specify the ground of objection with such particulars as are sufficient to indicate the matters relied on to make it out.

(b) Where an objection is made to an application for the issue or renewal of a certificate on the ground that the application does not give the information which the LA64 requires, or that the information is incomplete or inaccurate, or that the application is otherwise not in conformity with the LA64, it is sufficient for the objection to state the ground as a matter of suspicion, and to indicate reasons for the suspicion.

(c) When an objection to the application for the issue or renewal of a certificate is made and there appears to the court to be good reason to suspect that the application does not give the information required by the LA64 or the information is incomplete or inaccurate, or the application is otherwise not in conformity with the LA64, it is for the applicant to satisfy the court that the ground of objection cannot be made out, unless the applicant desires and is allowed to amend the application so as to remove the ground of objection.

(2) (a) An objection to an application for the issue or renewal of the certificate is made by lodging with the clerk to the magistrates two copies in writing of the objection not later than twenty-eight days after the application is made, or if the application is amended after the amendment is made.

The court may extend the time for the chief officer of police or the council to inspect the premises. In that case, the court must also extend the time for the police or council to make objections.

(*b*) On receipt of the objection to an application for the issue or renewal of a certificate, the magistrates' clerk must send a copy to the person signing the application at any address given by him for communications relating to the application. If there is no such address, the copy must be sent to the address given as that of the club.

The rules about lodging an objection, and the duties of the clerk with regard to notifying the applicant, apply in relation to any notice of intention to make representations as to conditions relating to the sale of liquor (see **8** below) in the same way as they apply to objection to an application for the issue or renewal of a certificate.

(*c*) Where an objection is made or a notice is given, the magistrates' court may make such order as it thinks just and reasonable for the payment of costs to the club by the person making the objection or giving the notice, or vice versa.

(*d*) Where the club applies for a renewal of a registration certificate in respect of different, additional or enlarged premises and a magistrates' court extends the time for objections, the court may order that the certificate to be renewed shall not continue in force (as it would otherwise do until the application was disposed of) beyond a day specified in the order.

(c) The hearing

(1) A magistrates' court may deal with an application of a club for the issue, variation or renewal of a certificate without hearing the club, but before refusing such an application, or renewing the certificate for a shorter period than is requested in the application, the court must give the club an opportunity to be heard. Moreover, before renewing a certificate for a longer period than one year, the court may invite any chief officer of police or local council to make representations.

(2) The club, if not represented by counsel or a solicitor, may be represented by the chairman or secretary, a member of the general committee or a duly authorised officer.

(d) Service of summons for cancellation or variation

(1) A summons issued on a complaint made against a club for the cancellation or variation of a certificate must be served on the chairman or secretary of the club, or the person who signed the last application for the issue or renewal of the certificate. This is

treated as service on the club. As well as being served on the club, the summons must be served on such persons, if any, as the magistrates issuing it direct.

(2) Where it appears to a court dealing with such a summons that it cannot be served on the club in the manner set out above, or not without undue difficulty or delay, the court may order that service on the club may be effected by serving the summons on a person whom it names, being a person who appears to the court to have, or to have had, an interest in the club or to be, or to have been, an officer of the club.

A complaint may be made against a club to cancel its registration certificate (on the ground that the club has not twenty-five members) notwithstanding that it is the complainant's case that the club does not exist.

7 Club rules

(a) Statutory requirements

The LA64 lays down a number of provisions about club rules (Sched 7). Where a club complies with them the court must make certain assumptions in the club's favour (see **1** above). It should be noted that a club is not compelled to bring its rules into conformity with these requirements, but if it does so the court must assume in the absence of objection that it is, eg 'established and conducted in good faith as a club'. Where a new club is applying for registration it is desirable that its rules should, if possible, conform to the requirements of the Schedule. The most important are:

(1) The affairs of the club in matters not reserved for general meetings or for discussion by the general body of members, must, under the rules, be managed by one or more elective committees (see Note (2) to **1** above for the meaning of 'elective committees'). One committee must be a general committee charged with the general management of affairs not assigned to special committees.

(2) There must be a general meeting of the club at least once a year, and fifteen months must not elapse without a general meeting.

(3) The general committee must be capable of summoning a general meeting at any time on reasonable notice.

(4) Any members entitled to attend and vote at a general meeting must be capable of summoning one or requiring one to be summoned at any time on reasonable notice, if a specified number of them join to do so; and the number required must

not be more than thirty nor more than one-fifth of the total of the members so entitled.

(5) At a general meeting the voting must be confined to members, and all members entitled to use the club premises must be entitled to vote, and must have equal voting rights. (However, the rules may exclude from voting, either generally or on particular matters members below a specified age (not greater than twenty-one), women (if the club is primarily a men's club) and men (if the club is primarily a women's club).) If the club is primarily one for persons qualified by service in the forces, the rules may exclude persons not so qualified from voting, either generally or on particular matters. If the rules allow for family membership they may exclude from voting any person taking the benefit of the rules as being a member of another person's family.

(6) Ordinary members must, under the rules, be elected either by the club in general meeting, or by an elective committee with or without other members added to it for the purpose and the name and address of any person proposed for election must be for not less than two days before the election prominently placed in the club premises or the principal club premises in a part frequented by the members.

(7) The rules must not make any such provision for the admission of members otherwise than as ordinary members, or in accordance with the rules required for ordinary members, above, as is likely to result in the number of members so admitted being significant in proportion to the total membership. (This is to prevent a club being largely composed of bogus 'special' members.)

As mentioned in **2** above, an application for a certificate must state or annex a statement of the rules of the club.

(b) Alterations (LA64, s 48)

Where any alteration is made in the rules of a club registered in respect of premises, the secretary of the club must give written notice of the alteration to the chief officer of police and to the clerk of the local authority. If the notice required is not given within twenty-eight days of the alteration, the secretary is liable to a fine at level 1 on the standard scale.

An application for renewal of a certificate must state any changes in the rules made since the last application, or that there have been no changes (see **2** above).

8 Sale of liquor by registered clubs (LA64, s 49)

Where a club is registered in respect of any premises, and the rules provide for admission to the premises of non-members and their guests and for the sale of liquor to them by the club for on-consumption, a licence is not required to cover such a sale. This is an exception to the general rule that a justices' licence is required to authorise the sale of intoxicating liquor. The object of the provision is to enable (for example) a golf club to sell liquor to visiting members of another club, without the device of making them into 'temporary members'. To prevent abuse, the court in deciding whether the club is 'established and conducted in good faith as a club' (see 1 above) may have regard to any provision in the rules for the sale of liquor by the club (LA64, s 49(2)).

The court may, when issuing or renewing a certificate, attach thereto such conditions restricting sales of liquor on the premises as it thinks reasonable. These may include conditions forbidding or restricting any alteration of the club rules so as to authorise sales not authorised at the time of the application to the court.

However, no such conditions may be attached so as to prevent the sale of liquor to a person admitted to the premises as being a member of another club if:

(1) the other club is registered in respect of premises in the locality which are temporarily closed; or

(2) both clubs exist for learned, educational, or political objects of a similar nature; or

(3) each of the clubs is primarily a club for persons who are qualified by service or past service, or by any particular service or past service, in Her Majesty's Forces and are members of an organisation established by Royal Charter and consisting wholly or mainly of such persons; or

(4) each of the clubs is a working men's club (that is, a club which is, as regards its purposes, qualified for registration as a working men's club under the Friendly Societies Act 1974, and is a registered society within the meaning of that Act or of the Industrial and Provident Societies Act 1965).

A certificate may be varied by imposing, varying or revoking any conditions restricting the sale of liquor on club premises. However, no such conditions may be imposed, varied or revoked except either:

(1) at the time of the renewal of the certificate; or

(2) on the application of the club; or

(3) on complaint in writing made against the club by the chief officer of police or the local authority.

At the hearing of an application for the issue or renewal of a certificate, or of the application by a club for the imposition, variation or revocation of a condition, the chief officer of police or the local authority are entitled, on giving written notice of intention to do so, to make representations as to the conditions which ought to be attached to the certificate in regard to sales of liquor at the club.

Where the rules of a club registered in respect of premises are altered so as to authorise sales of liquor at the premises not authorised by the rules at the time of the application or the last application by the club for the issue or renewal of a certificate, the alteration will not be effective to dispense with the requirement of a licence until notice of it has been given by the secretary to the chief officer of police and the clerk to the local authority. This must be done within twenty-eight days of the alteration.

9 The register of clubs (LA64, s 51)

The clerk to the justices is required to keep a register of clubs holding certificates. The register must show the hours on Sundays, Christmas Day and Good Friday, if any, fixed as the permitted hours by the club rules and any other particulars prescribed (LA64, s 51(2), as amended by LA88, Sched 1, para 1). It must be open on payment of the appropriate fee to inspection at all reasonable times. The police, the Customs and Excise authority, or an authorised officer of the local authority may inspect it without fee. The club must give written notice, signed by the chairman or secretary, to the clerk to the justices of any change in the particulars about the club which are contained or required to be contained in the register, and if the notice is not given within forty-two days of the change, both chairman and secretary are each liable to a fine at level 3 on the standard scale.

10 False statements, etc (LA64, s 53)

It is an offence if an application or notice by a club contains any statement known by the person signing it to be false in a material particular. It is also an offence if a person recklessly signs any application or notice which is so false. Imprisonment not exceeding three months, or a fine at level 3 on the standard scale, or both, may be imposed for this offence.

11 Appeals (LA64, s 50)

A club may appeal to the Crown Court against any decision of a magistrates' court:
(1) refusing to issue or renew a certificate; or
(2) cancelling a certificate; or
(3) as to the conditions of a certificate relating to sales of liquor; or
(4) prohibiting the use and occupation of premises for club purposes.

12 Inspection of premises (LA64, s 45)

Where a club applies for a certificate any constable authorised in writing may, on giving not less than forty-eight hours' notice to the applicant and (if the premises are not occupied by the club) to the occupier, enter and inspect the premises at any reasonable time on such a day as may be specified in the notice; the day may not be more than fourteen days after the making of the application. A council official authorised in writing has a similar right to enter and inspect the premises.

Where a club applies for the renewal of a certificate in respect of different, additional or enlarged premises, there is a similar right of inspection.

13 Fire authorities and clubs (LA64, s 46)

The local authority, if they are the fire authority, have similar rights in relation to the inspection of club premises on any application for the renewal of a certificate as they have in the case of an application for the issue of a certificate.

Where the local authority are not the fire authority, the justices' clerk must give the fire authority written notice of the making of an application for the issue or renewal of a certificate for any premises.

A fire authority other than the local authority have, in regard to any matter affecting fire risks, the same rights as a local authority in regard to the inspection of premises, and in regard to making objections to the issue or renewal of a certificate on the ground that the premises are not suitable and convenient for the purpose in view of their character and condition and of the size and nature of the club.

Note

Fire authority means the authority discharging in the area concerned the functions of a fire authority under the Fire Services Act 1947.

14 Search warrants (LA64, s 54)

If a magistrate is satisfied by information on oath that there is reasonable ground for believing:

(1) that there is ground for cancelling, in whole or in part, a club certificate and that evidence of it is to be obtained at the club premises; or

(2) that liquor is sold or supplied by or on behalf of a club in club premises for which the club does not hold a certificate or licence, or is kept in any club premises for sale or supply in contravention of the LA64,

he may issue a search warrant to the police authorising them to enter the club premises by force if need be and search them and seize any club documents. The search warrant remains valid for one month from its date.

15 Licensing of club premises (LA64, s 55)

The proprietor of a non-members' club has always been able to apply for a justices' licence authorising the sale of liquor in the club. Until the passing of the LA64 this was not open to a members' club, since the supply to members of liquor owned by the club does not constitute a 'sale' at law, and a licence would normally only be appropriate to authorise a sale. As we have seen, however, a members' club which does not wish or is unable to qualify for registration may now apply for a justices' licence in respect of its premises, notwithstanding that in law the supply of liquor on those premises is not and does not involve a sale (LA64, s 55). Under s 55, the club can apply for a justices' licence in respect of its premises (whether or not it is registered in respect of other premises), and where a club holds such a licence the rule forbidding liquor to be supplied at other than the premises registered does not apply.

Any justices' licence which is to be granted to a club must be granted in the name of an officer of the club nominated for the purpose by the club. A resolution of the club committee authorising the application together with documentary evidence of the nomination may be required. The rights and obligations of the licence holder relating to the sale of liquor and to licensed premises attach to the person in whose name the licence is, and they apply as if he were the holder of the licence in occupation of the premises. Any supply of liquor by the club to a member as such, or to any person on the order of a member, is treated for the purpose of the legislation governing the sale of liquor as a sale to the member.

Where a club is registered in respect of any club premises and application is made for the grant of a licence for other club premises of the club, the justices may not grant the licence unless satisfied that the purpose of the licence would not be served by the club being registered in respect of the other premises also, and that the grant of the licence is not likely to give occasion for abuse by reason of any difference in the permitted hours in the premises or otherwise. Where a justices' licence granted for club premises is subject to conditions forbidding or restricting the sale of liquor to non-members, the justices may insert in the licence a clause relieving the holder from compliance with enactments which require notices to be displayed in or on licensed premises, but do not apply to premises in respect of which a club is registered.

When the magistrates attach any conditions to a licence for club premises forbidding or restricting sales of intoxicating liquor to non-members, those conditions are disregarded in deciding whether a justices' on-licence is a restaurant licence, a residential licence or a residential and restaurant licence.

Note

Where a straightforward proprietary club is applying for a licence, it is generally simpler and better for the proprietor to make the application under s 3 of the LA64 in his own name, rather than under the provisions of s 55. Since it is the proprietor who will be making the sale, it is submitted that it is preferable for the licence to be in his name rather than in that of an 'officer of the club nominated for the purpose of the club'. In the case of proprietary clubs there is sometimes a fictional aspect to such 'nominations'. The purpose of s 55 is to enable such members' clubs as are not qualified for registration to be licensed.

Chapter 4

The Licensing of Gaming Clubs

1 The licensing system

The GA68 created a framework of control within which all forms of gaming which may become commercialised can be contained and supervised. In particular, it set up a system of licensing and registration by local justices for gaming clubs. Section 2 of the GA68 forbids gaming otherwise than on licensed or registered premises where any one or more of the following conditions are fulfilled:

(1) the game involves playing or staking against a bank whether the bank is held by one of the players or not;

(2) the nature of the game is such that the chances in the game are not equally favourable to all the players;

(3) the nature of the game is such that the chances in it lie between the player and some other person (or if there are two or more players lie wholly or partly between the players and some other person) and those chances are not as favourable to the player or players as they are to that other person.

The effect of this is to prohibit bankers' games and games which by their nature are not of equal chance, except on licensed and registered premises. However, this prohibition does not apply to such games when they take place on domestic occasions in private dwellings, or in such places as hostels. The gaming must not then be carried on as a trade or business; and the players must consist exclusively or mainly of persons who are residents or inmates in the establishment concerned.

Proprietary clubs offering gaming with some commercial or profitable element require to be licensed, while members' clubs require to be registered.

Note that 'gaming' is defined by s 52(1) of the GA68 as 'the playing of a game of chance for winnings in money or money's worth, whether any person playing the game is at risk of losing any money or money's worth or not'. 'Game of chance' does not include any athletic game or sport, but with that exception includes a game of chance and skill combined and a pretended game of chance and skill combined. In determining for the purposes of the GA68 whether a game which is played otherwise than against one or more other players is a game of chance and skill combined, the possibility of superlative skill eliminating the element of chance must be disregarded.

(a) The Gaming Board

The pivot of the system is the Gaming Board for Great Britain, referred to in this Chapter as 'the Board'. This is an entirely new body set up by the GA68, which has been well described as a kind of 'Statutory Jockey Club'.

It is the duty of the Board to keep under review the extent and character of gaming in Great Britain, and in particular to review the extent, character and location for gaming facilities which are for the time being provided in premises in respect to which licences under the GA68 are in force, or in respect of which clubs are registered under the GA68; or are the subject of applications for the grant or renewal of such licence or registration. However, the Board is under no duty to give a ruling upon the legality of a particular game: *Re de Keller's application* (1983) LS Gaz R 1491. The Board is a body corporate with perpetual succession, and has power to regulate its own procedure.

(b) Consent applications to the Board (GA68, Sched 2)

It is important to note that the licensing system is a two-stage one. The application itself is made to a committee of the justices for the district. This is the same committee as that which grants betting office licences under the BGLA63. But an application is of no effect unless the Board has issued to the applicant a certificate consenting to his application for a licence for the premises concerned. The certificate must still be in force at the time of the application, and the application must be made within the time specified on the certificate.

An application by the would-be holder of a licence for the Board's consent to an application for a licence is called a 'consent application'. Such an application must be made by the person proposing to make the relevant licence application, and must specify the premises in respect of which the relevant licence application is to be made, and also state whether that application will be for the grant of a bingo club licence, or for a licence under the GA68 other than a bingo club licence (see **6** and **21** below as to the distinction between these types of licence). A form of application for a consent certificate may be obtained from the Board, who issues with it printed notes and information for the guidance of applicants. The Board provides in its form GB1 a request for information on a number of points including details of the applicant, and the applicant's financial status, together with details of the proposed premises and the games to be played. The Board also requires to be provided with information of the financial requirements including estimates of capital expenditure and an estimate of cash floats and reserves necessary to operate the proposed gaming. In addition to form GB1 there are personal declaration forms (GB2) which have to be completed by an applicant or partner of an applicant, any director or secretary of an applicant company and any person who is providing financial backing or who will be in control of the business or the gaming at the club. The Board can call for such supporting documents as it considers are necessary. The Board may not issue a certificate if it appears to the Board that the applicant:

(1) not being a body corporate, is under twenty-one years of age; or

(2) not being a body corporate, is not resident in Great Britain or was not so resident throughout the period of six months immediately preceding the date on which the application was made; or

(3) being a body corporate is not incorporated in Great Britain.

In deciding whether to grant a consent application the Board has regard only to the question whether in its opinion the applicant is likely to be capable of and diligent in securing that the provisions of the GA68 and of any regulations made under it will be complied with; that gaming on the premises will be fairly and properly conducted; and that the premises will be conducted without any disorder or disturbance. In particular, the Board is required to take into consideration the character, reputation and financial standing of the applicant and of any person (other than the applicant) by whom if a licence were granted in the relevant licence application the club would be managed, or for whose benefit, if a licence were granted, the club would be carried on. However, the Board may also take into consideration any other relevant circumstances in determining whether the applicant is likely to be capable of and diligent in securing compliance with the Act and the other matters referred to above. The Board must act fairly by giving an applicant enough information of the objections against him to enable him to answer them. The Board does not need to give its reasons for refusal (*R v Gaming Board, ex parte Benaim and Khaida* [1970] 2 QB 417).

(c) Contents of certificate of consent

Where a certificate of consent has been issued it must specify the applicant and the premises concerned, specify a period within which the relevant licence application can be made, and state whether the consent is or is not limited to a bingo club licence.

2 Application for grant of licence (GA68, Sched 2)

An application may be made at any time. It must be in the form prescribed by the GCLR69; a specimen form appears at Appendix 9. The application is made to the clerk to the justices, and must specify by name and description a club which either:

(1) is a club for whose purposes the relevant premises are used at the time when the application is made, or are intended, if the licence is granted, to be used; or

(2) is intended, if the licence is granted, to be formed as a club for whose purposes the relevant premises will be used.

It must contain the particulars required by the GCLR69, and must, of course, be accompanied by a copy of the certificate of consent issued by the Board.

Not later than seven days after the date on which the application is made the applicant must send a copy of the application to:

(1) the Board;

(2) the appropriate officer of police;

(3) the appropriate local authority;

(4) the appropriate fire authority (if not the same as the appropriate local authority);

(5) the appropriate collector of duty.

Service of notices under the GA68 may be:

(1) by personal delivery; or

(2) by sending by post to the last-known or usual residence or place of business of the recipient in the United Kingdom; or

(3) in the case of a body corporate, by delivery to the secretary or clerk at the registered or principal office or by sending by post to the secretary or clerk at that office.

'Appropriate officer of police' means the chief officer of police for the police area in which the premises are or are to be situated. 'Appropriate local authority' means the local authority (being the council of a London borough, county district or the Common Council of the City of London) in whose area the relevant premises are or are to be situated. 'Appropriate fire authority' means the fire authority under the Fire Services Act 1947 in whose area the relevant premises are to be situated. 'Appropriate collector of duty' means the Collector of Customs and Excise for the area in which the relevant premises are or are to be situated. The address of this authority may be obtained from the Customs and Excise Department, King's Beam House, Mark Lane, London EC3R 7HE.

Not later than fourteen days after the making of the application the applicant must cause notice of the making of the application to be published by means of an advertisement in a newspaper circulating in the authority's area. The notice must specify the name of the applicant, the name of the club and the location of the premises, and indicate whether the application is for a bingo club licence or for a licence other than a bingo club licence. It must also state that any person who desires to object to the licence should send to the clerk to the authority, before such date, not being earlier than fourteen days after the publication of the advertisement, as may be specified in the notice, two copies of a brief statement in writing of the grounds of his objection.

Not later than fourteen days before the date specified in the notice the applicant must cause a like notice to be displayed outside the entrance to the premises and must take such steps as he reasonably can to keep the notice so displayed until that date. The notice published in the newspaper or displayed outside the entrance must not include any material not required by the provisions of the GA68.

Not later than seven days after the publication of the newspaper containing the advertisement the applicant must send a copy of the newspaper to the clerk to the authority; and the authority may not consider the application earlier than fourteen days after the date specified in the advertisement.

On or after the date so specified but not less than seven days before the date fixed by the authority for the consideration of the application, the clerk must send notice in writing of the date, time and place of the meeting of the authority at which the application will be considered:

(1) to the applicant;
(2) to all the persons and bodies concerned (ie the Board, police etc, see above); and
(3) if the clerk has received from any other person an objection in writing which has not been withdrawn, to that person.

The clerk must also cause notice of the meeting to be displayed at the place where the meeting is to be held in a position where it may conveniently be read by the public. With the notice to be sent by the clerk to the applicant of the time and place of the hearing, the clerk must send a copy of any objection which has not been withdrawn. Each licensing authority must hold four meetings each year; in January, April, July and October.

3 Application for renewal of licence (GA68, Sched 2)

An application for the renewal of a licence is to be made not earlier than five or later than two months before the date on which it is to expire. It must be made to the clerk to the authority in the form prescribed by the GCLR69. A specimen form appears at Appendix 10. However, the authority may entertain an application which is made later than on the proper date if they are satisfied that the failure to make it in time was due to inadvertence and if it is made before the end of such extended period as the authority may allow.

There are provisions for notifying the persons concerned of the application, similar to those relating to an application for a new licence. As to these, see para 13 of Sched 2 to the GA68. But *note* that a notice does not have to be displayed on the premises, and in this case it is the clerk who is required to advertise by newspaper.

4 Proceedings on application for grant or renewal

The authority may grant or renew the licence without hearing the applicant if no objection to the grant or renewal has been made by any person, or if every objection has been withdrawn, before the meeting. Otherwise the following persons are entitled to be heard by counsel or solicitor or in person:

(1) the applicant;

(2) any objector whose objection in writing has not been withdrawn; and

(3) any person who has made an objection out of due time whom the authority agree to hear. In such a case they may not hear the objection, unless the applicant requests otherwise, until the applicant has had time to consider a brief written statement of the grounds of objection.

Further, the justices must hear any representations made by or on behalf of the Board, the police, the local authority, the Commissioners of Customs and Excise or the fire authority.

The licensing authority have power to adjourn the consideration of any application for a grant or renewal from time to time for any purpose.

Evidence may be taken on oath, and the justices have power to make such order as they think fit for the payment of costs by the applicant to any objector, or by any objector to the applicant.

5 Grounds for refusal to grant or renew licence (GA68, Schcd 2)

The justices *may* refuse to grant a licence if it is not shown to their satisfaction that, in their area, a substantial demand already exists on the part of prospective players for gaming facilities of the kind proposed to be provided on the relevant premises.

Where it is shown to the satisfaction of the justices that such a demand already exists, the justices *may* refuse to grant a licence if it is not shown to their satisfaction that no gaming facilities of the kind in question are available in that area or in any locality outside that area which is readily accessible to the prospective players in question; or where such facilities are available, that they are insufficient to meet the demand.

The issue of 'demand' is usually the main one which the justices have to determine. The applicant in preparing his application must give careful consideration to proof of such 'demand'. In deciding whether existing facilities are sufficient the justices may consider the scale, type and quality of the facilities, as well as their quantity (*R v Manchester Crown Court, ex parte Cambos Enterprises Ltd* (1973) 117 SJ 222). Applicants will find it helpful to study the Annual Reports of the Board which deal with various aspects of 'demand'.

The Board may from time to time advise the justices as to the extent of the demand on the part of prospective players for gaming facilities of any particular kind, either generally in Great Britain or in any particular part of Great Britain, and as to the extent to which, and the places in which, gaming facilities of any particular kind are available. It will be recalled that it is one of the statutory duties of the Board to keep under review the extent, character and location of gaming facilities.

In deciding whether on an application for the grant of a licence it should be refused on the ground that there is no demand, the justices are required to 'take into account' (though not necessarily to act upon) any advice given by the Board as above, and must also take into account any representations which at the time when the application is being considered by them are made by or on behalf of the Board or any other person entitled to be heard.

Without prejudice to the power to refuse to grant a licence if no demand is shown, the justices *may* refuse to grant or renew a licence on any one or more of the following grounds:

(1) that the premises are unsuitable by reason of their layout, character, condition or location;

(2) that the applicant is not a fit and proper person to be the holder of a licence under the GA68;

(3) that, if the licence were granted or renewed, the club specified in the application would be managed by or carried on for the benefit of a person, other than the applicant, who would himself be refused the grant or renewal of a licence on the grounds that he is not a fit and proper person to be the holder of a licence;

(4) that the licensing authority, the Board, the police, the local authority or the fire authority, or their authorised representatives, have been refused reasonable facilities to inspect the premises;

(5) that any duty payable in respect of the premises under s 13 of the Finance Act 1966, or s 2 of or Sched 1 to the Finance Act 1970, or s 13 of or Sched 2 to the Betting and Gaming Duties Act 1972, or s 14 of or Sched 2 to the Betting and Gaming Duties Act 1981, remains unpaid;

(6) that any bingo duty payable in respect of bingo played on the premises remains unpaid.

Note

(1) Where the justices entertain an application for the grant or renewal of a licence under the GA68 in respect of any premises, and are satisfied that any bingo duty payable in respect of bingo played on the premises remains unpaid, they *must* refuse the application.

(2) Under Part II of the GCLR69 the justices may refuse to grant or renew a licence where the licence is to be in respect of premises to which a person might, otherwise than in an emergency, gain access directly from private premises not to be included in the licence.

'Premises' here includes any part of the premises and in particular any courtyard, lobby, passage or stairway. 'Private premises' include any premises to which the public have access (whether on payment or otherwise) only by permission of the owner, lessee or occupier. This ground of refusal, however, does not apply to licences to be granted or renewed subject to restrictions to be imposed limiting gaming to bingo, bridge or whist, or to both bridge and whist (see **6** below as to such restrictions).

(3) The justices must refuse to grant or renew a licence which is not to be subject to the above limitations where the licence is to be in respect of premises situated, wholly or in part, outside the area specified in the Gaming Clubs (Permitted Areas) Regulations 1971 (SI No 1538). The effect of this is that the justices must refuse to grant or renew a licence for 'hard gaming' where the relevant premises are not situated in an area where such gaming is permitted (see Appendix 11 for these areas).

In deciding whether the relevant premises are unsuitable by reason of their layout, character, condition or location, the justices are required to take into account any advice given by the Board.

The GA68, Sched 2 provides a further series of grounds, additional to those set out above, on which the justices may refuse to *renew* a licence. They are as follows:

(1) that it is not shown to their satisfaction that, in their area, a substantial demand exists on the part of the players or prospective players for gaming facilities of the kind proposed to be provided;

(2) that a person has been convicted of an offence under the GA68 in respect of a contravention, in connection with the premises, of any provision of the GA68 or of any regulations made under it;

(3) that while the licence has been in force the relevant premises have not been so conducted as to prevent disturbance or disorder;

(4) that while the licence has been in force gaming on the premises has been dishonestly conducted;

(5) that while the licence has been in force the relevant premises have been used for an unlawful purpose or as a resort of criminals or prostitutes (they *must* refuse to renew if the premises have been habitually used in these ways);

(6) that while the licence has been in force the appropriate precautions against the danger of fire have not been observed or have been insufficiently observed in the use of the premises.

The justices may also refuse to renew a licence on the ground that, within the period of twelve months ending with the date on which they consider the application, notice has been served on a person stating that a 'relevant certificate' issued in respect of him is revoked from the end of the period specified in the notice. The certificate referred to is the certificate of approval by the Board as to a gaming operative or manager being employed in a licensed club (see **20** below as to these certificates). A certificate is taken to have been a relevant certificate if it was one certifying that the person concerned had been approved by the Board in respect of the performance on the relevant premises of a function which, at the time when the notice referred to was served, he was authorised or required to perform on those premises in pursuance of a service agreement which was then in force; or in respect of his acting in relation to those premises in a capacity in which, at the time when that notice was served, he was acting or was authorised or required to act in relation to the premises.

The Board are given power to advise the justices on the question whether a substantial demand exists for gaming facilities of the kind proposed to be provided when they are arriving at their decision whether or not to renew a licence on this ground.

The justices *must* refuse to grant or renew a licence if a disqualification order is in force (see **11** below as to such orders).

Note that in a case where the justices have to decide whether the premises are unsuitable in respect of their location, and where the premises were used for the purpose of gaming during the period of a minimum of six months ending 19 December 1967, the justices *must* consider what (if any) evidence there is that those premises appeared to be unsuitable for that purpose during the period. Furthermore, if it appears to them that there is no evidence or insufficient evidence that they were unsuitable, the justices shall have regard in particular to that fact in deciding the question of suitability.

6 Restrictions on licence (GA68, Sched 2)

When granting or renewing a licence the justices may impose such restrictions (if any) on the hours during which gaming will be permitted to take place on the premises as appear necessary for the purpose of preventing disturbance or annoyance to the occupiers of other premises in the vicinity.

Further, the justices may impose restrictions of either or both of the following kinds:
(1) restrictions limiting the gaming to a particular part or parts of the premises;
(2) restrictions limiting the gaming to a particular kind of game or particular kinds of games.

Whether they impose restrictions of the above kind or not, the justices may also impose restrictions limiting the purposes, other than gaming, for which, while the licence is in force, the premises may be used. These restrictions may either be general or may relate to such times as are specified.

Where the justices grant a licence pursuant to a certificate of consent which states that the consent is limited to a bingo club licence, then when granting or renewing the licence the justices must impose restrictions limiting the gaming on the premises to bingo only.

Where the restrictions imposed limit gaming to bingo, no restrictions limiting the other purposes for which the premises may be used can be imposed. This is in line with the policy of the GA68 whereby clubs offering bingo only are encouraged to run other forms of entertainment (eg cabaret), as well as bingo.

Again, in considering whether to impose such restrictions, the justices are required to take into account any advice given them by the Board as well as any representations which are made, when the application is being considered, by or on behalf of the Board or any person entitled to be heard (eg the fire authority). Restrictions imposed under the above provisions are to be operative until the licence ceases to have effect or is next renewed, whichever is the first. The justices may impose similar or other restrictions on renewing the licence.

Under Part II of the GCLR69 the justices *must* (except in the case of a licence to be granted or renewed subject to restrictions limiting gaming to bingo, bridge or whist or to both bridge and whist) impose restrictions limiting gaming to the playing of games other than bingo.

They must also (except in such cases as above) impose a restriction limiting the purposes for which the premises may at any time be used to purposes other than dancing and the provision of music or entertainment by persons actually present and performing. The object here is to prevent premises used for 'hard gaming' being used also for dancing and live entertainment. Such 'mixed use' is considered to lead to the public being attracted to gaming by the provision of other entertainment. See, as to the Board's policy in this respect, the Board's Report for 1969.

7 Power to make regulations (GA68, s 22)

The Home Secretary is empowered by the GA68 to make regulations requiring the licence holder:

(1) to display in such manner and position as may be prescribed the rules in accordance with which any game is played on the premises, generally or in particular circumstances;

(2) to make, and retain during such period as may be prescribed, such records as may be prescribed respecting cheques given in exchange for cash or tokens to be used by players in gaming on

the premises, and with respect to redeemed cheques and substitute cheques within the meaning of GA68, s 16, and to provide such verification as may be prescribed of such records.

The Home Secretary may also make regulations imposing such prohibitions, restrictions or other requirements (in addition to those referred to above) as appear to him to be requisite:

(1) for securing that gaming on any premises licensed under the GA68 is fairly and properly conducted; or

(2) for preventing the use of any indirect means for doing anything which, if done directly, would be a contravention of the GA68 or any regulations made under it.

Further, the Home Secretary may make regulations providing that the justices:

(1) shall refuse to grant or renew a licence in such circumstances as may be prescribed by the regulations; or

(2) may refuse to grant or renew a licence in such circumstances as may be so prescribed, without prejudice to any other grounds on which the grant or renewal might be refused; or

(3) shall, in such circumstances as may be prescribed in the regulations, impose restrictions limiting the gaming to a particular part or parts of the premises or limiting the gaming to a particular game or kind of game.

The Home Secretary may also by regulation impose restrictions with respect to the hours during which gaming will be permitted to take place on licensed premises.

Note

The Gaming Clubs (Licensing) Regulations 1969 (SI No 1110), the Gaming Clubs (Prohibition of Gratuities) Regulations 1970 (SI No 1644), the Gaming Clubs (Permitted Areas) Regulations 1971 (SI No 1538), as amended, the Gaming Clubs (Hours and Charges) Regulations 1984 (SI No 248) and the Gaming (Records of Cheques) Regulations 1988 (SI No 1251) have been made under these provisions.

8 Notification of the Board's advice (GA68, Sched 2)

The clerk to the justices must, at the request of any applicant for the grant or renewal of a licence, furnish him with a statement setting out any advice given to the justices by the Board which the justices propose to take into account in determining the application.

9 Appeals (GA68, Sched 2)

(a) Appeals by applicant

Where the justices refuse to grant or renew a licence, or they impose restrictions upon it, the clerk to the justices must give notice of the decision to the applicant. Within twenty-one days of the date of the service of the notice the applicant may, by giving notice to the clerk, appeal against the decision to the Crown Court. On receiving notice of appeal the clerk is required to send notice to the Crown Court, together with a statement of the decision against which the appeal is brought, and giving the name and last known residence or place of business of the applicant and any objector. The Crown Court then gives to the applicant, to the Board, to the police, to the excise authority and to any person who opposed the application, as well as to the justices not less than fourteen days' written notice of the date, time and place appointed for the hearing of the appeal.

The Crown Court may allow or dismiss the appeal or reverse or vary any part of the decision of the justices whether the appeal relates to that particular part or not. The Crown Court may, in fact, deal with the application as if it had been made to it in the first instance. The judgment of the Crown Court is final.

(b) Costs of appeal

The Crown Court has power to make such order in relation to the costs of an appeal as it thinks just. See the Crown Court Rules 1982 (SI No 1109).

(c) Appeal by the Board

Where the justices grant or renew a licence after hearing any objection or representation made by the Board or any other person, and the Board desire to contend that the licence ought not to have been granted or renewed, or that on granting or renewing the licence the licensing authority ought to have imposed restrictions or (where restrictions were imposed) ought to have imposed more stringent restrictions, the Board may appeal.

A similar procedure is then followed to that adopted in appeals by the applicant.

10 Revocation by the Board of certificate of consent (GA68, Sched 2)

The Board may at any time revoke a certificate of consent which they have granted. They may do so whether the applicant has by then obtained a licence or not. Subject to their powers referred to in the next paragraph, the Board may not revoke a certificate of consent in respect of any premises unless it appears to them:

(1) that if the holder of the certificate were then applying for one the Board would be precluded from issuing a certificate on the ground that the holder, not being a body corporate, was under twenty-one, or was not resident in Great Britain, or was not so resident throughout the period of six months immediately preceding the date of the application, or being a body corporate, was not incorporated in Great Britain; or

(2) that any information which in, or in connection with, the application on which the certificate was issued, was given to the Board by or on behalf of the applicant was false in a material particular; or

(3) that, since the certificate was issued, a licence held by the holder of the certificate (in respect of the same *or* different premises) has been cancelled by a disqualification order or otherwise (see **11** below as to such orders).

These are all 'factual' grounds for revocation. The GA68 envisages that once a certificate has been granted the holder shall not be kept in peril of it being revoked except in certain defined circumstances, for instance where an outsider who has gained effective control of the club is himself not a fit person to hold a licence. The GA68 thus provides that the Board may revoke the certificate of consent held by a licence holder at any time if it appears to them that in relation to the conduct of the premises or the conduct of gaming there the effective control is being exercised by a person other than the holder of the certificate, and that the other person in question, in view of his character and reputation, is not a person to whom, if he were then applying for a certificate of consent, the Board would issue such a certificate.

When the Board determine to revoke a certificate of consent in this way they must serve a notice on the holder stating that the certificate is revoked from the end of the period of eight weeks from the date of service of the notice, and the revocation takes effect from the end of that period. However, the Board may serve on the holder, before the end of the period, a further notice stating that they have rescinded their decision to revoke it. When serving such a notice the Board are also required to send a copy to the clerk to the justices, to the police and to the excise authority.

The revocation of a certificate in this way has the effect of making the licence of no effect. The GA68 provides that when a certificate is thus revoked any licence in respect of the premises concerned which specifies that certificate as being the certificate in pursuance of which the application for the licence was made, and is in force at the time when the revocation of the certificate takes effect, at once ceases to be operative.

11 Cancellation of licence (GA68, Sched 2)

(a) Applications to cancel

Any person may at any time apply to the justices to cancel a licence. The application must be in the form prescribed in the GCLR69, and be accompanied by two copies of a statement of the grounds on which the application is made. The GA68 provides that when he receives such an application the clerk to the justices must submit it to one of the justices. If that single justice, after considering the application, considers that further consideration of the matters referred to in the statement accompanying the application is unnecessary or inexpedient before the time when the renewal of the licence falls to be considered, or the licensing authority would be required to refuse the application to cancel on the ground that it was made for reasons which have been, or ought properly to have been, raised previously by way of objection when the licence was granted or on renewal, he is required to cause notice in writing to be given to the applicant that the application is refused. The applicant, however, may raise the matters of objection on renewal.

In all other cases the single justice to whom the application is submitted must refer it to the full bench of justices. The clerk must then give to the applicant for cancellation, to the holder of the licence, to the police, to the Board and to the excise authority not less than twenty-one days' notice in writing of the date, time and place appointed for the consideration of this application. He must also send to the licence holder a copy of the applicant's statement of the grounds on which the application is made. The justices then consider the application at one of their meetings and the applicant for cancellation and the licence holder are entitled to be heard either in person or by counsel or solicitor. The GA68 envisages that some of these applications may be made by the police, but whether or not the applicant is the chief officer of police, the justices must hear any representations made by him or any person authorised on his behalf. As in the case of an application for a licence, the justices have full power to adjourn consideration of the application to cancel if they see fit. Evidence may be given on oath. The justices also have power to order costs to be paid by the applicant for cancellation, or by the licence holder.

The justices *must* refuse the application if satisfied that it is made on grounds which have been, or ought properly to have been, raised previously by way of objection either when the licence was granted or on an occasion when it was renewed. In other circumstances the justices have a discretion to cancel the licence on any of the grounds specified in **5** above as grounds for refusing to grant or renew a licence. If they cancel the licence, the cancellation does not take effect until the expiration of time for appeal; and if the licence holder does appeal cancellation does not take effect until the appeal has been determined or abandoned. The rules for appeal against cancellation are the same as those for appeal against refusal to grant or renew (see **9** above).

A special power is given to the Board to appeal against the decision of the justices to the Crown Court if the justices refuse to cancel a licence.

(b) Cancellation on conviction

If the licence holder is convicted of certain statutory offences (as set out in Sched 2 to the GA68), and the Commissioners of Customs and Excise certify that the conviction is a second or subsequent conviction for such an offence committed in relation to gaming on the premises concerned, and while the same person has been the holder of the gaming club licence, the magistrates' court must order that the licence be cancelled, if the Customs and Excise Department apply for this to be done.

When a licence is cancelled under these provisions the clerk of the court concerned must, unless he is also the clerk to the justices who are the licensing authority for gaming club licences (as in many cases he will be), send a copy of the order to the clerk to the relevant justices. They must then refuse any application by the licence holder for the grant of a licence in respect of the same or any other premises if it is made less than twelve months after the date of the order of cancellation. The clerk must also notify the Board of the cancellation.

(c) Disqualification on cancellation of licence

When a licence is cancelled by the justices, as the result of an application for such cancellation, the justices have power to make a disqualification order prohibiting such a licence from being held in respect of the premises during a specified period. This period must not exceed five years from the date when the order comes into force. If a disqualification order is made any licence within the prohibition, if previously obtained, is cancelled; and if one is subsequently obtained it is null and void.

Where the justices cancel a licence, and make a disqualification order, the licence holder has a right of appeal to the Crown Court similar to his right of appeal against cancellation.

(See **22** below as to disqualification orders made by a court on conviction of any person for contravention of the GA68.)

12 Form of licence (GA68, Sched 2)

The form of licence is prescribed by the GCLR69. It must specify by name and description the club which was referred to in the application for the licence, and specify, in a manner sufficient to identify it, the certificate of consent in pursuance of which the application was made.

If restrictions are imposed on a licence by the justices the licence as granted or renewed must include a statement of the restrictions.

13 Duration of licence (GA68, Sched 2)

A licence, if not renewed, ceases to be in force at the end of the period of one year beginning with the date on which it was granted; or, if renewed, it shall unless further renewed cease to be in force at the end of the period of one year from the date on which it would otherwise have expired.

Where an application for the renewal of a licence has been duly made the licence does not cease to be in force before the justices have determined the application. Where the justices refuse to renew a licence it does not cease to be in force before the time within which the applicant can appeal against the refusal has expired (see **9** above). If he does appeal, the licence does not cease to be in force until the appeal has been determined or abandoned.

14 Death of licence holder (GA68, Sched 2)

If a licence holder dies while the licence is in force, the licence does not cease to be in force before the end of the period of six months beginning with the date of his death; and except for the purposes of renewal, the personal representatives are deemed to be the holders of the licence. The justices have power from time to time on the application of the personal representatives to extend or further extend the period for which the licence continues to be in force, if they are satisfied that the extension is necessary for the purpose of winding up the deceased's estate and that no other circumstances make it undesirable.

15 Transfer of licence (GA68, Sched 2)

(a) Consent to transfer

Subject to the justices' consent, a licence may be transferred from one person to another (not from one set of premises to another) at any time. But an application for a transfer has no effect unless the Board have issued to the applicant a certificate consenting to his applying for a transfer of the licence. The application to transfer must be made within the period specified in the certificate.

The Board must not issue a certificate on any such application if it appears to them that the person to whom the licence is proposed to be transferred:

(1) not being a body corporate, is under twenty-one years of age; or

(2) not being a body corporate, is not resident in Great Britain or was not so resident throughout the period of six months immediately preceding the date on which the application was made; or

(3) being a body corporate, is not incorporated in Great Britain.

In deciding whether to issue such a certificate of consent the Board must have regard only to the question whether, in their opinion, the proposed transferee is likely to be capable of, and diligent in, securing that the provisions of the GA68 and of any regulations made under it will be complied with, that gaming on the premises specified will be fairly and properly conducted, and that the premises will be conducted without disorder or disturbance.

The Board must also take into consideration the character, reputation and financial standing of the proposed transferee and of any person by whom, if the licence were transferred to the proposed transferee, the club would be maintained, or for whose benefit, if the licence were transferred, the club would be carried on.

The Board may also take into consideration any other circumstances which appear to them to be relevant in deciding whether the proposed transferee is likely to be capable of and diligent in securing the above matters.

If the Board issue a certificate consenting to the application for a transfer, the certificate must specify the period within which the application to the justices for the transfer can be made. The Board may revoke the certificate at any time before the licence has been transferred, but must not do so unless it appears to them either that any information which, in or in connection with the application on which the certificate was issued, was given to the Board by or on behalf of the applicant was false in a material particular; or that since the certificate was issued a licence under the GA68 held by the proposed transferee has been cancelled by virtue of a disqualification order.

If the Board decide to revoke a certificate by virtue of these provisions they must serve a notice on the holder of the certificate stating that the certificate is revoked. The revocation takes effect upon the service of the notice.

(b) Application for transfer

As we have seen, applications for the transfer of a licence from one person to another may be made at any time. But a certificate of consent by the Board is first required. The application for transfer must be made to the clerk of the justices in the form prescribed in the GCLR69 and must be accompanied by a copy of the certificate of consent issued by the Board for the purposes of the application.

(c) Notice of application

Not later than seven days after the date on which the application is made, the applicant must send a copy of the application to:
(1) the Board;
(2) the police;
(3) the local authority; and
(4) the excise authority.
See paras 58–61 of Sched 2 to the GA68 for other requirements as to the application.

(d) Refusal of transfer

On an application for the transfer of a licence, the justices may not refuse the transfer except on the grounds:
(1) that the person to whom the licence is proposed to be transferred is not a fit and proper person to be the holder of a licence;
(2) that, if the licence were transferred to that person, the club specified in the licence would be managed by or carried on for the benefit of a person who would himself be refused a grant of

a licence on the ground that he is not a fit and proper person to be the holder of one; or

(3) that any duty payable by the intended transferee under s 13 of the Finance Act 1966, or s 2 of or Sched 1 to the Finance Act 1970, or s 13 of or Sched 2 to the Betting and Gaming Duties Act 1972 or s 14 of or Sched 2 to the Betting and Gaming Duties Act 1981, or any bingo duty payable by him remains unpaid.

There is a right of appeal by the applicant or the Board against refusal to transfer a licence; and by the Board against the grant of a transfer which it has opposed.

16 Payment of fees (GA68, s 48)

No licence may be granted, renewed or transferred except on payment by the applicant to the clerk to the justices of the fees chargeable. The fees are laid down in s 48 of the GA68, as amended by regulation from time to time. Enquiry should be made of the clerk to the justices to ascertain the proper fee in each case.

17 Notification of change of directors (GA68, Sched 2)

Where the holder of a licence is a company or other body corporate and a change occurs in the persons who are directors or in the persons in accordance with whose directions or instructions the directors are accustomed to act, the company or other body must as soon as reasonably practicable after the time of change serve on the clerk to the justices, the police and the Board, a notice giving particulars of the change. A fine at level 3 on the standard scale is laid down for an infringement of this provision.

18 Relinquishment of licence (GA68, Sched 2)

The holder of a licence may at any time relinquish it by giving notice to the clerk to the justices. Where such notice is given, the licence is treated as cancelled. The clerk to the justices must then give notice of the fact of relinquishment to:

(1) the Board;
(2) the police;
(3) the local authority;
(4) the fire authority (if not the same as the local authority);
(5) the excise authority.

19 Registration of members' clubs for gaming (GA68, Sched 3)

The GA68 provides for the registration rather than the licensing of members' clubs where gaming is carried on. A members' club is one where the property belongs to all the members jointly. It differs from a proprietary club in that in the latter the property belongs to a proprietor, the members being allowed to use the premises and property by virtue of payment of a subscription. The justices are the authority for granting registration as they are for granting licences.

Registration is also appropriate for miners' welfare institutes as well as for members' clubs. A miners' welfare institute is one organised for the social well-being and recreation of persons employed in or about coal mines (or of such persons in particular), where either the institute is managed by a committee or board of which not less than two-thirds consists partly of persons appointed by or on the nomination of, or appointed or elected from among persons nominated by, British Coal, and partly of persons appointed by or on the nomination of, or appointed or elected from among persons nominated by, an organisation or organisations representing persons so employed; or the premises of the institute are held on trusts to which s 2 of the Recreational Charities Act 1958 applies. In this book the word 'club' is used to cover both clubs and institutes.

The registration system is intended to be 'precautionary' only; it is meant for those genuine members' clubs which wish to provide gaming as a subsidiary activity, and either to allow unequal chance games like pontoon to be played, or to make a small charge for play to recover their costs. The object of registration is to verify the club's credentials; and to impose conditions sufficient, but no more, to prevent the club from being captured and exploited by commercial interests.

(a) Application for registration (GA68, Sched 3)

The application for registration is on the same lines as the application for a licence. The application must be made to the clerk to the justices in the form and manner prescribed by the GCLR69, and specify by name and description a club which either is a club for whose purposes the relevant premises are used at the time when the application is made, or are intended, if the licence is granted, to be used; or is intended, if the licence is granted, to be formed as a club for whose purposes the relevant premises will be used. The application is made in the same way as an application for a licence (see **2** above). However, the following differences should be noted in the requirements as to the application:

(1) a certificate of consent by the Board does not have to be obtained;
(2) the notice to be published does not have to state whether the application is for a bingo club only;
(3) there is no requirement to display a notice on the premises;
(4) it is not necessary to give notice to the fire authority or the local authority.

Note that it is required that a copy of the application should be sent to the Board. A number of clubs have in the past overlooked this obligation.

(b) Renewal of registration (GA68, Sched 3)

Here again the procedure generally follows that laid down for an application for a licence (see **2** above).

(c) Proceedings on applications (GA68, Sched 3)

The same rules apply in regard to the hearing of these applications as apply to the hearing of applications for licences (see **2** above). However, the fire authority and local authority are not entitled to make representations unless they are objectors.

(d) Grounds for refusal (GA68, Sched 3)

The justices *must* refuse to register or renew the registration of a club if it appears to them that the club is not a bona fide members' club; or has less than twenty-five members; or is of merely temporary character.

Further, the justices must refuse to register a club or to renew its registration if it appears to them that the principal purpose for which the club is established or conducted is gaming, unless they are satisfied that the gaming in question consists exclusively of playing bridge or whist or both bridge and whist.

These are the only grounds for refusal of first registration, the intention of the Act being that a members' club, once its bona fides is established, is entitled to registration.

The justices *may* refuse to register a club where the club has previously been registered and either its registration has been cancelled; or an application for renewal of registration has been refused.

The justices may refuse to renew the registration of a club on any one or more of the following grounds (in addition to those specified above):
(1) that a person has been convicted of an offence under the GA68

in respect of a contravention in connection with the relevant premises of any of the provisions of the GA68 or regulations made under it;

(2) that, while the club has been registered, the relevant premises have not been so conducted as to prevent disturbance or disorder;

(3) that, while the club has been so registered, gaming on the premises has been dishonestly conducted;

(4) that, while the club has been so registered, the relevant premises have been used for an unlawful purpose as a resort of criminals or prostitutes;

(5) that any duty in respect of the premises under s 13 of the Finance Act 1966, or s 2 of or Sched 1 to the Finance Act 1970, or s 13 of or Sched 2 to the Betting and Gaming Duties Act 1972, or s 14 of or Sched 2 to the Betting and Gaming Duties Act 1981, remains unpaid;

(6) that any bingo duty payable in respect of bingo played on the premises remains unpaid.

Note

Where the justices entertain an application for the renewal of registration and are satisfied that any bingo duty payable in respect of bingo played on the premises remains unpaid they must refuse the application.

Further the justices *must* refuse to renew a registration if satisfied that, while the club has been registered, the premises have been habitually used for an unlawful purpose or as a resort of criminals or prostitutes.

(e) Restrictions imposed on registration (GA68, Sched 3)

On registering or renewing the registration of a club the justices may, if they think fit, impose restrictions limiting the gaming to a particular part or parts of the premises. This may be necessary to ensure that the gaming continues to be an 'ancillary' activity of the club. Any restrictions so imposed have effect until the registration of the club ceases to have effect or is next renewed (whichever first occurs). This is without prejudice to the power of the justices, where the registration is renewed, to impose the like or other restrictions on renewal.

(f) Appeals (GA68, Sched 3)

Where the justices refuse to register or renew the registration of a club or impose restrictions upon it, the clerk must give notice of the decision to the applicant. The applicant, within twenty-one days of the date of service of the notice, may appeal against the decision to the Crown Court. The rules set out at **9** above as to appeals in respect of the refusal to grant or renew a licence apply also to appeals in respect of registration.

Where the justices register or renew the registration of a club after hearing any objection or representation made by or on behalf of the Board or any other person, and the Board wish to contend that the registration or renewal ought to have been refused, the Board may appeal against the decision to the Crown Court.

(g) Cancellation of registration (GA68, Sched 3)

The rules as to cancellation of a licence set out at **11** above apply also to cancellation of registration. On any application for the cancellation of registration the justices may cancel the registration on any of the grounds set out at (*d*). Where an application for cancellation is made, and the justices decide to cancel the registration, the clerk to the justices must at once give notice of the decision to the chairman or secretary of the club, and within twenty-one days from the date of service of that notice, the chairman or secretary may by notice to the clerk to the justices appeal against the decision to the Crown Court.

Where an application for cancellation of the registration is made by the Board and the justices refuse to cancel it, the Board may by notice to the clerk appeal to the Crown Court.

If a person is convicted of an offence in the categories set out at (*d*), and the Commissioners of Customs and Excise certify that the conviction is a second or subsequent one for such an offence committed (whether by the same or some other person) in relation to gaming on the premises concerned while the club has been so registered, and apply to the court for an order, then the justices must order that the registration of the club shall be cancelled.

Note, however, that an order made under these provisions is not to have effect until the end of the period within which notice of appeal may be given. If notice of appeal is given, the order does not have effect until the appeal has been determined or revoked. If the appeal is allowed, the order has no effect. Where registration is cancelled by virtue of such an order, the clerk to the court making it must send a copy to the clerk to the justices concerned with the registration of the club. Those justices must refuse any application for the registration of that club in respect of the same or any other premises if it is made less than twelve months after the date of the order.

(h) Issue and duration of certificates of registration (GA68, Sched 3)

Where a club is registered, or its registration is renewed, the justices must issue a registration certificate in the prescribed form. The certificate must state any restrictions imposed by the justices upon it. Registration, if not renewed, ceases to have effect at the end of the period of one year beginning with the date on which it was effected. If renewed, registration, unless further renewed, ceases to have effect at the end of the period for which it was renewed or last renewed.

An application for renewal of registration may specify a number of years, not exceeding ten, for which the renewal is requested; the justices may renew the registration for a term of years not exceeding that specified in the application. Otherwise, renewals of registration are for a period of one year. Where registration has been renewed for a period of two or more years, and is subject to any restrictions imposed by the justices, and where it is desired to cancel or vary the restrictions, an application for renewal may be made in any of the years comprised in the term notwithstanding that the registration is not due to expire in that year.

Note that where on application the justices refuse to renew registration, it does not cease to have effect before the time within which the applicant can appeal. If he appeals, the registration does not cease to have effect until the appeal has been determined or abandoned.

(i) Relinquishment of registration (GA68, Sched 3)

A club may at any time relinquish its registration by giving notice to the clerk of the justices. The registration is then treated as cancelled.

Where the registration is relinquished in this way the clerk to the justices must give notice of the fact to the Board, the police and the excise authority.

20 Approval by the Board of gaming operatives (GA68, s 19)

Section 19 of the GA68 requires gaming operatives employed in licensed clubs to be certified by the Board as approved in respect of such employment. The Board also have power to require the certification of any person engaged in a managerial or supervisory capacity. No person may in pursuance of any service agreement perform any function specified below unless a certificate has been issued by the Board, and is in force, certifying that he has been approved by the Board for the performance of that function.

The functions concerned are:

(1) taking part in the gaming as a player (ie no employee of the club may take part in the gaming unless certified); or

(2) assisting the gaming by operating or handling any apparatus, cards, tokens or other articles used in the gaming; or

(3) issuing, receiving or recording cash or tokens used in the gaming or cheques given in respect of any such cash or tokens or in respect of sums won or lost in the gaming; or

(4) watching (otherwise than as manager, organiser or supervisor) the gaming or the performance by any person in pursuance of any service agreement of any of the above functions.

Thus all croupiers, invigilators or similar persons must be certified as approved by the Board.

Note that this does not apply to operatives in bingo clubs, in whose case relevant functions are prescribed by regulation, and not by the GA68.

The Board may also serve a special notice in respect of any licensed club premises on any person appearing to the Board to be acting in any capacity as manager, organiser or supervisor in relation to the gaming or in relation to employees who perform any of the above functions. Such a notice requires the person concerned before the end of the specified period (not less than twenty-one days from the date of service) to obtain the approval of the Board to his acting in relation to the club premises in any of these capacities. After the end of the specified period, the person concerned must not act in such capacity in relation to the club premises unless a certificate has been issued by the Board certifying that he has been approved for acting in that capacity.

(a) Procedure (GA68, Sched 5)

The application for a certificate of approval is made to the Board. It must specify the premises of the club and the function or capacity in respect of which the certificate is required. In deciding whether to issue a certificate the Board must have regard only to the question whether, in relation to the premises specified, the applicant is a fit and proper person to perform the function or to act in the capacity concerned. Where it appears to the Board that the applicant requires their approval in respect of his performing the function, or acting in the capacity, in question in relation to all or any of a number of premises specified in the application, and the Board decide to give that approval, they may, if they think fit, issue him a single certificate specifying all the premises for which he is approved. A certificate continues in force until revoked by the Board.

(b) Revocation of certificate

The Board may at any time revoke a certificate if it appears to them that, in relation to the premises specified, the person concerned is not a fit and proper person to perform the function or act in the capacity concerned. The Board must serve a notice on the person to whom the certificate relates stating that the certificate is revoked as from the end of the period of twenty-one days from the date of service of the notice. The revocation takes effect from the end of the period.

(c) Certain applications effective pending determination

Note that when an applicant applies for a certificate of approval and either at the time of the application a certificate issued by the Board in respect of him is in force (whether in relation to the same premises or not); or the certificate is required by reason of a special notice having been served upon him by the Board (that is, a notice to someone acting in a managerial, organising or supervisory capacity), and the application is made before the end of the period specified in the Board's notice, the application has the same effect as a certificate until it is determined by the Board. The applicant can thus carry out the duties concerned pending the determination of his application for approval.

21 Bingo clubs (GA68, s 20)

The GA68 distinguishes bingo clubs, where only bingo is played, from other forms of gaming club, and accords them favourable treatment.

The phrase 'bingo club premises' is used to mean premises in respect of which a licence is in force and where, by virtue of restrictions imposed on the licence, gaming is limited to bingo.

(a) 'Linked bingo'

This type of bingo, played simultaneously on different sets of premises, would prima facie be a contravention of the requirement of the GA68 that no person shall participate in gaming if he is not present on the premises at the time (s 12(1)). The GA68 provides that 'linked bingo' is permissible. Where a game is played at the same time on different bingo club premises, and:

(1) all the players take part in the same game at the same time and all are present at that time on one or other of the premises; and

(2) the draw takes place on one or other of those premises while the game is being played; and

(3) any claim of one of the players to have won is indicated to all the other players before the next number is called;
then, if the conditions set out below are fulfilled, the different sets of premises are treated as being the same.

The necessary conditions are:

(*a*) The aggregate amount paid to players as winnings must not exceed the aggregate amount of the stakes hazarded by the players; and

(*b*) there must be a limit on total prize money of £3,500 in any one week. The Secretary of State has power to vary this limit by regulation.

(b) 'Multiple bingo'

Under the Gaming (Bingo) Act 1985, provision is made for multiple bingo. It is defined as a game of bingo played jointly on different bingo club premises where:

(1) the draw is determined before the beginning of the game by its organiser and announced on each premises while the game is being played;

(2) the game is played on each premises within a specified period which is the same for all of them;

(3) each player competes for a prize calculated by reference to the stakes hazarded at all those premises and also for either or both of:

(*a*) a prize calculated by reference to the stakes hazarded at a group of those premises which includes the premises on which the player is taking part in the game; and

(*b*) a prize calculated by reference to the stakes hazarded at the last mentioned premises.

Further provision is made to modify GA68, s 12 (which restricts persons who may participate in gaming). The maximum prize is £50,000. The game organiser must hold a certificate of approval from the Board, applications for which are dealt with in the Schedule to the Act, as is revocation of the certificate. The Gaming Clubs (Multiple Bingo) Regulations 1986 (SI No 834), made under s 3 of the Act, state that the number of multiple bingo games that may be played at any bingo club premises in a twenty-four hour period shall be one, and that the game shall last no longer than thirty minutes.

(c) Other provisions

Bingo clubs also enjoy a relaxation in the rules providing for an interval between application for and admission to membership. In other gaming clubs the rule is that a person may only take part in gaming as a member if not less than forty-eight hours previously he has either applied for membership or given written notice, in person at the premises, of his intention to take part in gaming (GA68, s 12). A member of a bingo club may take part in gaming if twenty-four hours have elapsed since he applied for membership; furthermore, he does not have to give the notice in writing as to intention to take part in gaming.

Further, persons under eighteen may be present in the room while bingo is being played if they do not take part in the game as players.

As we have seen, bingo club operatives only require to be approved by the Board if carrying out functions of a kind to be prescribed by regulation.

The aggregate amount paid to players as winnings in respect of all games of bingo played in any one week on any particular bingo club premises must not exceed the aggregate amount of the stakes hazarded by the players by more than £1,500, but this sum is variable by regulation. 'House prizes'—those offered by the proprietor from his own resources—are thus permissible to a modified extent.

Application for membership of a bingo club may be made otherwise than in person at the club premises.

22 Disqualification orders (GA68, ss 24, 25)

Where a person is convicted of an offence under s 23(1) and (2) of the GA68 (which deals with contraventions of the rules for gaming) the court by which he is convicted may make a disqualification order prohibiting a licence from being held in respect of the premises where the offences were committed during a period specified in the order. The period must not exceed five years from the date when the order comes into force. Where a disqualification order is made, any licence within the prohibition obtained before the order was made, or before it took effect, is cancelled as from the time when the order takes effect. Any licence obtained after the order is null and void.

Note that a disqualification order does not take effect until the end of the period within which the person on whose conviction the order was made can appeal against the conviction or against the making of the order. If he does appeal, it does not take effect until the appeal has been determined or abandoned. The court may not make an order prohibiting the holding of a licence in respect of premises specified in the order unless an opportunity has been given to any person interested in the premises and applying to be heard to show cause why the order should not be made.

A disqualification order may at any time during the period of disqualification be revoked or varied by reducing the period concerned. If an application is made for the revocation or variation of a prohibition of this kind a copy of the application must be served on the chief officer of police for the police area in which the premises are situated.

Note that a disqualification order made by the Crown Court, on appeal from a decision of the magistrates' court, is treated as having been made by the magistrates' court for the purposes of an application to revoke or vary it. Such an application should therefore be made to the magistrates' court, and not to the Crown Court.

23 Restrictions on games to be played (GA68, s 13)

As we have seen Part I of the GA68 (which deals with gaming elsewhere than on premises licensed or registered under the GA68) forbids gaming, except in a domestic situation, where the game involves playing or staking against a bank, whether the bank is held by one of the players or not; or the nature of the game is such that the chances of the game are not equally favourable to all the players; or the nature of the game is such that the chances in it lie between the player and some other person, or (if there are two or more players) lie wholly or partly between the players and some other person, and those chances are not as favourable to the player or players as they are to that other person. Thus bankers' games and games which by their nature are not of equal chance are prohibited. This prohibition is also applied by s 13 of the GA68 to gaming on premises licensed or registered under the Act; but regulations may be made providing that this prohibition shall not have effect in relation to any gaming if the game played is of a kind specified in the regulations, and is so played as to comply with such conditions as may be prescribed by the regulations in relation to that kind of game. Regulation 2 of the Gaming Act (Registration under Part II) Regulations 1969 (SI No 550), provides that s 13 is not to have effect in relation to pontoon and chemin-de-fer played on premises so registered. The Gaming Clubs (Bankers' Games) Regulations 1970 (SI No 803), allow roulette, dice, baccarat and blackjack to be played on licensed premises, and lay down the manner in which those games may be played.

Chapter 5

The Licensing of Betting Offices

Ready money off-course betting was made legal by the Betting and Gaming Act 1960, which allowed the establishment of 'betting shops'. However, in order to run such an establishment it is necessary to obtain a betting office licence. The grant of such licences is now governed by the BGLA63, Sched 1.

1 The licence

Licences are granted by a committee of justices consisting of not less than five or more than fifteen of the justices acting for the area. This committee is known as the 'appropriate authority', and is referred to in this book as 'the authority'. The authority must fix for each year a day in January, April, July and October as the day when it will hold a meeting for considering applications for betting office licences. Only three classes of person may apply for a betting office licence, namely:

(1) a person who is for the time being the holder of or an applicant for a bookmaker's permit;

(2) the Totalisator Board;

(3) a person who, not being the holder of or an applicant for a bookmaker's permit, is for the time being both:

(*a*) accredited by a bookmaker who is the holder of a bookmaker's permit or by the Totalisator Board as an agent for the purpose of receiving or negotiating bets by way of business with a view to those bets being made with that bookmaker or, as the case may be, with or through that Board; and

(*b*) the holder of, or an applicant for a permit (known as a 'betting agency permit') authorising him to hold a betting office licence (BGLA63 s 9(2)).

Note
(1) A betting office licence may be applied for notwithstanding that the premises have still to be constructed, or are still in the course of construction (BGLA63, s 9(3)).
(2) A bookmaker's permit is a permit granted by the authority to enable a person to act as a bookmaker on his own account. Such a permit is required whether the bookmaker carries on business on a racecourse, a dog-track or in a licensed betting office. The procedure for application for a permit is similar to that for a licence.
(3) A betting agency permit is a permit authorising its holder to hold a betting office licence. The holder must be accredited by a bookmaker who holds a bookmaker's permit, or by the Totalisator Board, as an agent for receiving or negotiating bets by way of business with a view to these bets being made with the bookmaker or with or through the Board. Such permits are granted by the same authority as that which grants betting office licences and bookmaker's permits; the procedure for an application is similar. This book, however, deals only with applications for betting office licences; as it is these which are more usually opposed before the authority.

2 The application

An application for the grant of a licence can be made at any time. It must be made to the clerk to the justices in whose area the 'relevant premises' are or are to be situated. The relevant premises are those premises in respect of which the application is made. While the application can be made at any time, the authority is only required to consider such an application on the days specified in the months referred to above. They *may*, however, hold a meeting on any other day for the purpose of considering applications.

(a) Form

The application must be in the form laid down by the Betting (Licensing) Regulations 1960, as amended. A specimen form of application is shown at Appendix 7.

(b) Notices

(1) Not later than seven days after making an application for a licence the applicant must send a copy of his application to the

chief officer of police for the police area where the relevant premises are or are to be situated.

(2) Within the same period the applicant must send a copy of the application to the appropriate local authority. This means the council (being the council of a London borough or county district, or the Common Council of the City of London) within whose area the relevant premises are situated.

(3) The applicant must also, within the same period, send a copy of the application to the Collector of Customs and Excise for the area. The address may be obtained from the Customs and Excise Department, King's Beam House, Mark Lane, London EC3R 7HE.

(4) Not later than fourteen days after the making of the application the applicant must cause an advertisement of it to be published in a newspaper circulating in the authority's area; although this can be in a local newspaper it is usually placed in one of the racing dailies such as *Sporting Life*. The notice must state that anyone who desires to object to the grant of the licence should send to the clerk of the authority before such date not earlier than fourteen days after the publication of the advertisement as may be specified in the notice two copies of a brief statement of the ground of his objection.

(5) The applicant must also cause a like notice to be posted up outside the entrance or the site of the proposed entrance to the premises not later than fourteen days before the date so specified, and take such steps as he reasonably can to keep that notice so posted until that date.

(6) Not later than seven days after the publication of a newspaper containing the advertisement the applicant must send a copy of the newspaper to the clerk to the authority. The authority may not consider the application earlier than fourteen days after the date specified in the advertisement. Not earlier than such date and not less than seven days before the date appointed for consideration of the application the clerk must send notice in writing of the date, time and place of the meeting of the authority at which the application will be considered:

(*a*) to the applicant;

(*b*) to the chief of police;

(*c*) if the clerk has received from any person an objection in writing which has not been withdrawn, and the address of that person is known to the clerk, to that person;

(*d*) to the Collector of Customs and Excise.

The clerk must also cause notice of that meeting to be displayed at the place where the meeting is to be held in a position where the notice can be conveniently read by members of the public, and in sending notice to the applicant the clerk must include a copy of any objection to the grant which has been received from the police, the local authority or any other person.

(c) Service of documents

Where any notice or other document is required to be given or sent to any person by the clerk or by the Crown Court the requirement is satisfied if the document is either served personally on that person or sent to him by post at his usual or last-known residence or place of business in the UK, or in the case of a company at the registered office.

3 Proceedings before the authority

The authority may grant the licence without hearing the applicant and without a formal hearing if no objection to the grant has been made, or if every objection has been withdrawn before the beginning of the meeting. Otherwise any of the following may be heard in person, or by counsel or a solicitor:

(1) the applicant;
(2) any person for whom an objection which has not been withdrawn was received by the clerk before he sent out the notice referred to above;
(3) the person making any other objection which the authority has decided to hear. Where a person fails to send in an objection within the due time, the authority *may* refuse to entertain it. They *must* not hear it, unless the applicant requests otherwise, until the would-be objector has given to the clerk and the applicant a brief statement in writing of the grounds of his objection, and the applicant has had time to consider it. The authority must also hear any representations made otherwise than by way of objection by the police or Customs and Excise.

Note

The authority may take evidence on oath. The usual procedure is for the applicant to open his case and call his witnesses. The objectors then present their evidence and address the authority on their objections. The applicant may be accorded a right of reply if the authority so directs, but this is not always done. A plan showing the existing betting offices within a radius of half a mile or one mile of the proposed new licensed premises is often produced by the applicant to assist the authority. The clerk should be consulted as to the authority's normal requirements about this.

The authority may make such order as they think fit for the payment of costs by or to the applicant or by or to any objector whose objection was not withdrawn before the day on which the clerk sent out the notices.

4 Grounds for refusal of grant

The authority *must* refuse the grant of a betting office licence if they are not satisfied:

(1) where the applicant is not the Totalisator Board, that on the date from which the licence would come into force the applicant will be the holder of a bookmaker's licence or betting agency permit; and

(2) that the premises are or will be enclosed; and

(3) that there are or will be means of access between the premises and a street otherwise than through other premises used for the effecting with persons resorting to those other premises of transactions other than betting transactions.

The authority *may* refuse the application on the ground:

(1) that having regard to the lay-out, character, condition or location of the premises, they are not suitable for use as a licensed betting office; or

(2) that the grant or renewal would be inexpedient having regard to the demand for the time being in the locality for the facilities afforded by licensed betting offices and to the number of such offices for the time being available to meet that demand;

or

(3) that the premises have not been properly conducted under the licence (this only applies in the case of renewals of existing licences, as to which see **6** below).

Note

Ground (2) above, relating to 'demand', is the most common ground for refusing the grant of a licence. An applicant should come to court prepared to prove that 'current demand' exists. Proving demand may involve a consideration of a number of factors including some or all of the following:

(1) an analysis of the area;

(2) maps to show the locality and the existing facilities;
(3) support from local witnesses both persons resident in the area and persons working there;
(4) development changes;
(5) any increase in population;
(6) consideration of existing facilities and especially if they are overcrowded or inconvenient either in terms of the service they provide or their location.

The authority when refusing an application must state the ground of its refusal.

5 Appeals

When the authority refuse to grant a licence they must forthwith notify the applicant of the result, and within twenty-one days of being so notified the applicant may appeal to the Crown Court against the refusal. An objector has no right of appeal against the grant: nor have the police. As soon as practicable after receiving the notice of appeal the clerk must send the notice to the Crown Court, with a statement of the decision against which the appeal is brought, and the name and last-known residence or place of business of the appellant and of any person who opposed the application before the authority. The Crown Court officer then enters the appeal, and gives not less than seven days' notice in writing to the appellant, the appropriate officer of police, the Customs and Excise, any person who opposed the application before the authority, and to the authority, of the date, time and place appointed for hearing the appeal.

The Crown Court may by its order either:
(1) confirm the refusal; or
(2) on payment by the appellant to the appropriate officer of the Crown Court for transmission to the clerk of the authority of the appropriate fee, grant or renew the licence in the same way as the authority would have done.

The judgment of the Crown Court is final. A justice may not act on the hearing or determination of an appeal from any decision in which he took part.

6 Renewal of licence

(a) Procedure

The authority must in February in each year give in writing to the holders of licences which fall to be renewed in that year, and cause to be published, by means of a newspaper advertisement circulating in the area, notice of a day in April on which they will hold a meeting for the purpose of considering applications for renewal. The notice must include the time and place appointed for the meeting and state:

(1) in the case of the notice given to the licence holder, that any such application must be received by the clerk to the authority before a specified date, being a date not earlier than fourteen days after both the giving of the notice in writing and the publication of the advertisement;

(2) in the case of the notice by advertisement, that any person who desires to object to the renewal of any particular licence shall send to the clerk of the authority before the same date two copies of a brief statement in writing of the grounds of his objection.

Any application for the renewal of a licence must be made to the clerk before the date specified in the notice. It must be in the form prescribed by the Betting Licensing Regulations 1960. A specimen form is given at Appendix 8. Not earlier than that date nor later than seven days before the day in April appointed by the notice for the consideration of renewals, the clerk:

(1) if he has received from any person an objection in writing to the renewal of a particular licence, being an objection which has not been withdrawn, and the address of the person concerned is known to the clerk, must send to that person a notification as to whether or not an application for the renewal of the licence has been made;

(2) must send to the person making the application to renew a copy of any objection to the renewal which he has received from the police, the local authority or any other person, which has not been withdrawn.

(b) Grounds for refusal to renew

These are the same as the grounds set out above for refusing to grant a licence.

(c) Appeal against refusal to renew

There is a right of appeal to the Crown Court against a refusal to renew. The procedure is the same as that for an appeal against the refusal of a grant.

7 Duration of licence

A licence must show the date with effect from which it is to be or is to be continued to be in force. Unless renewed or further renewed it normally ceases to be in force at the end of 31 May falling not less than three nor more than fifteen months after the date so shown. The licence is not transferable.

Where an application for renewal has been made, so far as lies within the applicant's control, the licence does not cease to be in force before the authority makes its determination on the application. If the authority refuses to renew a licence the licence continues in force until the end of the period allowed for an appeal. If an appeal is made it continues until the appeal is determined or abandoned. Where a licence holder dies, the licence continues in force for six months and his legal personal representatives are deemed to be the holders of it. The authority may from time to time, on the representatives' application, further extend the time, if they are satisfied that the extension is necessary for the purpose of winding up the deceased's estate and that no other circumstances make it undesirable.

Chapter 6

Lotteries

A lottery is a scheme for distributing prizes by lot or chance. If merit or skill comes into the distribution, the scheme is not a lottery.

The law on lotteries was altered and extended by the Lotteries Act 1975. That Act was superseded by the Lotteries and Amusements Act 1976, which consolidated the BGLA 63 and most of the Lotteries Act 1975. It is referred to in this book as 'the LAA'. It provides in particular for the promotion of lotteries by any local authority, and any society concerned with charitable, sporting, cultural or other non-commercial purposes.

Generally, all lotteries which do not constitute gaming are unlawful. 'Gaming' here has the same meaning as in the GA68 (see Chapter 4). There are, however, four types of 'excepted lottery' which are lawful if conducted in accordance with the LAA. They are:

(1) small lotteries incidental to 'exempt entertainments';
(2) private lotteries;
(3) societies' lotteries;
(4) local lotteries.

1 Small lotteries incidental to exempt entertainments (LAA, s 3)

An 'exempt entertainment' is a bazaar, sale of work, fete, dinner, dance, sporting or athletic or other entertainment, whether limited to one day or extending over two or more days. A lottery promoted as an incidental of such a function is not unlawful; but the statutory conditions must be observed. These are:

(1) The whole proceeds of the entertainment (including those of the lottery) after deducting:
   (*a*) the expenses of the entertainment, excluding expenses incurred in connection with the lottery; and
   (*b*) the expenses incurred in printing tickets in the lottery; and

(*c*) such sum (if any), not exceeding £50, or such other sum as may be specified in an order made by the Secretary of State, as the promoters think fit to appropriate on account of any expenses incurred by them in purchasing prizes in the lottery,

must be devoted to purposes other than private gain.

(2) None of the prizes must be money prizes.

(3) Tickets or chances must not be sold or issued, nor must the result be declared, except on the premises where the entertainment takes place and during its progress.

(4) The facilities for participating in lotteries under this section of the LAA, or those facilities together with any other facilities for participating in lotteries or gaming, must not be the only, or the only substantial, inducement to persons to attend the entertainment.

2 Private lotteries (LAA, s 4)

A private lottery is one in Great Britain which is promoted for, and in which the sale of tickets or chances by the promoters is confined to, either:

(1) members of one society established and conducted for purposes not connected with gaming, betting or lotteries; or

(2) persons all of whom work on the same premises; or

(3) persons all of whom reside on the same premises;

and which is promoted by persons each of whom is a person to whom tickets may lawfully be sold. In the case of a lottery promoted by the members of a society, each must be a person authorised in writing by the society's governing body to promote the lottery.

Note

Each local or affiliated branch or section is regarded as a separate and distinct society for this purpose.

Private lotteries are not unlawful: but the statutory conditions must be observed in connection with their promotion and conduct. These are:

(1) The whole proceeds, after deducting only expenses incurred for printing, and stationery, must be devoted to the provision of prizes for purchasers of tickets or chances, or, in the case of a lottery promoted for the members of a society, must be devoted either:

(*a*) to the provision of prizes as aforesaid; or

(*b*) to purposes which are purposes of the society; or

(*c*) partly to the provision of prizes and the remainder to such purposes.

(2) There must not be exhibited, published or distributed any written notice or advertisement of the lottery other than:

(*a*) a notice exhibited on the premises of the society, or on the premises on which the persons for whom it is promoted work or reside; and

(*b*) such announcement or advertisement of it as is contained in the tickets, if any.

(3) The price of every ticket or chance must be the same, and the price must be stated on the ticket.

(4) Every ticket must bear on the face of it the name and address of each of the promoters, a statement of the persons to whom the sale of tickets or chances is restricted, and a statement that no prize won in the lottery shall be paid or delivered to any person other than to persons to whom the winning ticket or prize was sold; and no prize must be paid or delivered except in accordance with that statement.

(5) No ticket or chance must be issued or allotted by the promoters except by way of sale, and on receipt of its full price, and no money or valuable thing so received must in any circumstances be returned.

(6) No tickets must be sent through the post.

3 Societies' lotteries (LAA, s 5)

A society's lottery is one promoted on behalf of a society established and conducted wholly or mainly for one or more of the following purposes:

(1) charitable purposes;

(2) participation in or support of athletic sports or games or cultural activities;

(3) other purposes which are neither purposes of private gain nor purposes of any commercial undertaking.

Note

Any purpose for which a society is established and conducted, and which is calculated to benefit the society as a whole, is not to be held to be a purpose of 'private gain' by reason only that action in its fulfilment would result in benefit to any person as an individual.

A society's lottery is not unlawful if:

(1) it is promoted in Great Britain;
(2) the society is registered with the 'registration authority'. This means, in England, a London borough council, a district council, the Common Council of the City of London or the Council of the Scilly Isles; and in Wales, a district council. It must be the authority in whose area the office or head office of the society is situated;
(3) it is promoted in accordance with a scheme approved by the society;
(4) either the total value of tickets or chances to be sold is £10,000 or less, or the scheme is registered with the Gaming Board before any tickets or chances are sold.

Thus a society intending to promote lotteries is required first to register itself with the local council; and also to register its lottery scheme with the Board if its lotteries are to have a turnover of more than £10,000.

Note

(1) The whole proceeds of a society's lottery after deducting sums lawfully appropriated on account of expenses or for the provision of prizes must be applied to purposes of the society.
(2) The amount of the proceeds of a society's lottery appropriated for the provision of prizes must not exceed one half of the whole proceeds of the lottery.
(3) The amount of the proceeds of a society's lottery appropriated on account of expenses (exclusive of prizes) must not exceed whichever is the less of:
   (*a*) the expenses actually incurred; and
   (*b*) whichever of the amounts specified below applies.

The relevant amounts are:

(1) where the whole proceeds of the lottery do not exceed £10,000, 25 per cent of those proceeds; or
(2) where the whole proceeds exceed £10,000, 15 per cent of those proceeds or such larger percentage not exceeding 25 per cent as the Gaming Board may authorise in the case of a particular lottery. The Board takes the view that Parliament intended that lottery expenses should be kept to a minimum, and should form a declining proportion of the proceeds as the proceeds increase. It has issued Notes for Guidance, showing the maximum expenses likely to be authorised in relation to the proceeds of a particular lottery (eg when the proceeds are £20,000 the maximum expenses likely to be authorised are £3,750). See

pamphlet GBL6, 'Registration of Lottery Schemes', issued by the Board.

(a) Returns (LAA, Sched 1, Part II)

Schedule 1 to the LAA requires certain returns to be rendered to the registration authority by the promoters of a society's lottery. The promoter must, not later than the end of the third calendar month after the date of the lottery, send to the authority a return, certified by two other members of the society, being persons of full age appointed in writing by the governing body, showing:

(1) a copy of the scheme under which the lottery was promoted;
(2) the whole proceeds of the lottery;
(3) the sums appropriated out of those proceeds on account of expenses and prizes respectively;
(4) the particular purpose or purposes to which the proceeds were applied in pursuance of s 5(4) of the LAA (which requires the whole proceeds, after deduction for expenses and prizes, to be applied to purposes of the society) and the amount applied for that purpose, or for each of those purposes, as the case may be; and
(5) the date of the lottery.

Note

The above rules do not apply to a society's lottery promoted in accordance with a scheme registered with the Board.

(b) Registration of societies (LAA, Sched 1, Part I)

The rules for registration with the local authority of societies wishing to promote lotteries are contained in Sched 1 to the LAA. The application must specify the purposes for which the society is established and conducted. Except as mentioned below, the local authority (ie the council) *must* register the society on an application duly made, and notify the society in writing that it has done so. However, the local authority *may* refuse or revoke registration (after giving the society the opportunity of being heard) if it seems to the authority:

(1) that any person has been convicted of an offence as specified in the Schedule (see below), committed in connection with a lottery promoted or proposed to be promoted on behalf of the society; or
(2) that the society does not satisfy or has ceased to satisfy the

statutory conditions (ie if it is not established and conducted for one or more of the specified purposes).

Note

(1) The specified offences include the 'general lottery offences' set out in s 2 of the LAA and any offence involving fraud or dishonesty.
(2) There is an appeal to the Crown Court against the refusal or revocation of registration.

4 Local lotteries (LAA, ss 6, 7, 8)

A local lottery is one promoted by a local authority. A local lottery is not unlawful if:

(1) it is promoted in Great Britain; and
(2) it is promoted in accordance with a scheme approved by the local authority; and
(3) the scheme is registered with the Gaming Board before any tickets or chances are won.

Thus, local authorities, while not subject to local registration requirements (as are societies in respect of their lotteries) *must* register a scheme with the Board, no matter how small their lotteries are to be. As to the contents of such schemes, see **7** below. A 'local authority' means: in England, a county council, a district council, a London borough council, the Common Council of the City of London, the Council of the Scilly Isles and a parish council; in Wales, a county council, a district council, and a community council.

A local authority may promote a local lottery for any purpose for which they have power to incur expenditure under any enactment. There are provisions making it the duty of a local authority to give such publicity to the object (ie the particular purpose or purposes for which the lottery is promoted) as will be likely to bring it to the attention of persons purchasing tickets or chances. Unless the Secretary of State consents to a different course, money accruing from a local lottery must be applied to the declared object. The Secretary of State may only give his consent if satisfied with one of the matters set out in LAA, s 7(4) (eg that the object in whole or in part has been as far as may be fulfilled).

The local authority are required to pay the whole proceeds of a local lottery, after deducting the expenses of promoting it, and the sum required for prizes, into a separate 'lottery fund'. Any money in such a fund is to be invested, and any income credited to the fund.

Note

The rules set out at **3** above in relation to the amount permitted to be appropriated on account of expenses for societies' lotteries apply also to local lotteries.

5 Frequency of lotteries

No society or local authority may hold more than 52 lotteries in any period of twelve months, but:

(1) when the date of two or more society's lotteries promoted on behalf of one society is the same and the total value of the tickets or chances to be sold in those lotteries does not exceed £45,000, all those lotteries are to be treated as one; and

(2) when the date of two or more lotteries promoted by one local authority is the same and the total value of the tickets or chances to be sold in the lotteries does not exceed £45,000, all the lotteries are to be treated as one.

The date of any lottery promoted on behalf of a society must be not less than seven days after the date of any previous lottery promoted on behalf of that society, except that the date of a lottery promoted for the purpose of selling tickets or chances wholly or mainly to persons attending a particular athletic or sporting event may be less than seven days after a previous lottery promoted on behalf of the society.

The date of any lottery promoted by a local authority must be not less than seven days after the date of any previous lotteries promoted by that authority.

6 Registration of lottery schemes with the Gaming Board (LAA, Sched 2)

As we have seen, a lottery scheme must be registered with the Board by a society, if the society's lotteries are to have a turnover of more than £10,000 and all local lottery schemes must be so registered. The rules for such registration are contained in Sched 2 to the LAA. The Board must register a scheme submitted to them unless:

(1) in the case of a scheme submitted by a society, the society is not registered with the local authority (see above); or

(2) the scheme is contrary to law; or

(3) except where the Secretary of State otherwise directs, the Board is not satisfied:

    (*a*) that all lotteries promoted by or on behalf of the applicant within the last five years have been properly conducted;

(*b*) that all fees payable under the LAA have been paid;

(*c*) that all requirements of the Board as to the provisions of accounts and information have been complied with;

(4) except where the Secretary of State otherwise directs, it appears to the Board that an unsuitable person will be employed in connection with the promotion of a lottery under the scheme.

Note

(1) The Lotteries Regulations 1977 (SI No 256) specify the contents of lottery schemes and contain further provisions as to the sale of tickets and otherwise. The rules as to the contents of such schemes are set out at **7** below.

(2) The Board has issued Notes for Guidance (see their pamphlet GBL6, 'Registration of Lottery Schemes'), which will be of assistance to applicants for registration.

(3) An 'unsuitable person' means one who has been convicted of certain offences specified in the Schedule. These include the general lottery offences specified in s 2 of the LAA and any offence involving fraud or dishonesty.

The Board have power to revoke the registration of any scheme on any of the grounds (1), (2), (3) or (4) referred to above. They also have power to revoke the registration of any scheme where it appears to them an unsuitable person (see above) has been employed for reward in connection with the promotion of any lottery under the scheme. Revocation does not have effect in relation to any lottery in respect of which any tickets or chances have already been sold at the date of revocation. The Secretary of State has power to restore any registration which the Board may have revoked on any of the grounds referred to under (3) or (4) above. The Board further have power to require the provision of accounts in relation to any lottery promoted under a registered scheme, and any other information which they may require in respect of any lottery promoted or to be promoted under a scheme registered by them or submitted to them for registration. In the exercise of these powers, they require the provision of a skeleton account in respect of each lottery held under a registered scheme.

7 Contents of lottery schemes (Lotteries Regulations 1977: SI No 256)

The following rules apply to the contents of a lottery scheme submitted to the Board.

(1) The scheme must specify the name and address of the society or local authority by which the scheme was approved.

(2) In the case of a society's scheme, the scheme must specify the following matters relating to the registration of the society with the local authority (see **3** above) (as we have seen, local lotteries do not require such registration):

(*a*) the name and address of the registration authority;

(*b*) the date of registration;

(*c*) the reference number (if any) of the registration.

(3) The scheme must specify the period during which it is to have effect, and in such a way as to secure that the scheme does not have effect for a period of more than three years.

(4) The scheme must specify:

(*a*) in the case of a scheme having effect for less than twelve months, the number of lotteries which may be promoted under it; and

(*b*) in any other case, the number of lotteries which may be promoted under it in any period of twelve months;

and in either case the scheme must require that the number so specified shall not be exceeded.

(5) (*a*) The scheme must specify a proportion (not exceeding one half) as being the proportion of the whole proceeds of any lottery under the scheme which may be appropriated for the provision of prizes in that lottery; and must require that the proportion so specified shall not be exceeded except in the special circumstances mentioned below.

(*b*) The special circumstances are that:

(i) the proceeds of the lottery fall short of the sum reasonably estimated; and

(ii) the appropriation is made to fulfil an unconditional undertaking as to prizes given in connection with the sale of the relevant tickets or chances; and

(iii) the total amount appropriated in respect of prizes does not exceed the amount which could have been appropriated out of the proceeds of the lottery if the proceeds had amounted to the sum reasonably estimated.

(6) In the case of a scheme approved by a local authority, the scheme must make provision as to whether all or any class of:

(*a*) members of the society; and

(*b*) officers of the authority

are to be precluded from buying tickets or chances in any lottery under the scheme, or not.

8 'Instant' lotteries

The date of a lottery is defined by s 23 of the LAA as the date on which the winners in the lottery are ascertained. This definition gives rise to difficulties in the case of 'instant' lotteries, where the winners are not ascertained by a 'draw' but by reference to details printed on the ticket. These details are often concealed by a coating which the purchaser of the ticket scrapes off to reveal the printing. In such a case, where tickets are sold over a period, there could be said to be several 'dates' for each lottery. The Board have expressed the view (see Report of the Gaming Board for Great Britain 1977) that the 'date' of the lottery in such a case is to be taken as the last day on which tickets are to be on sale. Where in what is initially an 'instant lottery' the winner of the major prize is ascertained by a 'draw' at the conclusion of the lottery, the date of the draw is, in the Board's view, the 'date' of the lottery.

9 Rules for authorised lotteries (LAA, s 11)

The following rules apply as indicated to societies' and local lotteries.
(1) In the case of a society's lottery:
   (*a*) the promoter must be a member of the society authorised in writing by the governing body of the society to act as promoter; and
   (*b*) every ticket and every notice or advertisement of the lottery lawfully exhibited, distributed or published must specify the name of the society, the name and address of the promoter and the date of the lottery.
(2) No ticket or chance in a society's lottery or a local lottery is to be sold at a price exceeding £1.00.
(3) The price of every ticket or chance must be the same and the price must be stated on the ticket.
(4) No person must be admitted to participate in a society's lottery or a local lottery in respect of a ticket or chance except after payment to the society or authority of the whole price of the ticket or chance, and no money received for or on account of a ticket or chance must in any circumstances be returned.
(5) No prize in a society's lottery where the total value of tickets or chances to be sold is £10,000 or less may exceed £2,000 in amount or value.
(6) The scale of lotteries allowed under the LAA depends on their

frequency, and lotteries are categorised for this purpose (see below). No prize in a society's lottery where the scheme is registered with the Board, or in a local lottery, is to exceed in amount or value the sum specified below as 'the appropriate sum' in relation to that lottery.

(7) The 'appropriate sum' is:
   (a) £6,000 for a 'short-term lottery';
   (b) £9,000 for a 'medium-term' lottery;
   (c) £12,000 for any other lottery.

Note

'Short-term lotteries' are lotteries where less than one month has passed since the date of any previous lottery.

'Medium-term lotteries' are lotteries where less than three months, but not less than one month, have passed since the date of any previous lottery.

(8) The total value of tickets or chances sold in a society's lottery, where the scheme is registered with the Board, or in a local lottery, is not to exceed 'the appropriate sum' in relation to that lottery.

(9) The appropriate sum is:
   (a) £45,000 for a short-term lottery;
   (b) £90,000 for a medium-term lottery;
   (c) £180,000 for any other lottery.

(10) The amount of the proceeds of a society's lottery or a local lottery appropriated for the provision of prizes is not to exceed one half of the whole proceeds.

(11) The 'appropriate sums' referred to above may be varied by regulation.

10 Societies' lotteries: summary

For ease of reference, a list of the statutory requirements in respect of a society's lottery is set out below:

(1) The society must be established and conducted for charitable, sporting, cultural or other non-commercial activities.

(2) The society must be registered with the local council.

(3) The lottery must be promoted in accordance with a scheme approved by the society.

(4) If the total value of tickets or chances to be sold exceeds £10,000 the scheme must be registered with the Board.

(5) The whole proceeds, after deducting sums lawfully appro-

priated on account of expenses or to provide prizes, must be applied to the society's purposes.

(6) The promoter must be a member of the society authorised in writing by the governing body.

(7) Every ticket, notice or advertisement must specify the name of the society, the name and address of the promoters and the date of the lottery.

(8) No ticket or chance must be sold at a price exceeding £1.00.

(9) The price of every ticket or chance must be the same.

(10) The price must be stated on the ticket.

(11) No person must participate except after payment of the whole price of his ticket or chance.

(12) No money received for a ticket or chance must be returned.

(13) The rules as to maximum prize money and as to the total value of tickets or chances must be observed.

(14) The rules as to frequency of lotteries must be observed.

(15) The amount of the proceeds appropriated for the provision of prizes must not exceed one half of the whole proceeds.

(16) The rules as to the amount of the proceeds appropriated on account of expenses (exclusive of prizes) must be observed.

(17) No ticket or chance must be sold to anyone under sixteen.

(18) No ticket or chance must be sold to a person in any street (but sales by a person present in a kiosk or shop premises having no space for the accommodation of customers are permitted).

(19) No ticket or chance must be sold to a person:
  (a) in any licensed betting office;
  (b) in any premises used wholly or mainly for providing amusements in the form of amusements with prizes or amusements by way of slot machines, or both; or
  (c) in any bingo or other gaming club.

(20) No ticket or chance must be sold by means of a vending machine.

(21) No ticket or chance must be sold by a person when visiting any other person at his home in the discharge of any official, professional or commercial function not connected with lotteries.

(22) The rules as to rendering returns to the registration authority must be observed (see **3** above).

(23) No ticket or chance may be sold or distributed or offered for sale more than three months before the date of any previous society's lottery promoted on behalf of the same society.

(24) Every ticket must specify the name of the registration authority with which the society is registered.

(25) Where the information on the ticket or a notice of advertisement of a society's lottery includes any reference to a person who for reward is or has been acting or assisting in the promotion of the lottery, the size of lettering used in such reference must not exceed the size of the smallest lettering used to specify the name of the society; and that reference must be given no greater prominence than the name.

(26) No request or requirement shall be made to any person supplying lottery tickets of the prescribed kind to the effect that they shall be supplied in such a manner or so marked as to enable a ticket to be identified before it is sold in the lottery as a winning ticket. (The 'prescribed kind' of tickets are those manufactured or designed so as to conceal such information appearing in or on the ticket by way of words, figures, signs, symbols or other features as would, if revealed, indicate that the ticket is a winning ticket or not. 'Winning ticket' means one which when sold in a lottery entitles the holder to claim a prize.)

(27) No prize may be offered on terms that winning it depends on the purchase of more than one ticket or chance.

Note

Items (17) to (21) and (23) to (27) above are contained in the Lotteries Regulations 1977 (SI No 256), as amended.

11 Agents

Some societies and local authorities employ agents to conduct their lotteries. The LAA contains no provision as to the employment of agents; and so long as their fees do not cause lottery expenses to exceed the statutory limits, and responsibility for the lottery remains with the society or local authority, the employment of agents appears to be permissible.

Chapter 7

Application to the Divisional Court

Two types of application can be made in licensing cases to the Divisional Court:
(1) by way of judicial review;
(2) by way of case stated.
These applications may only concern decisions made on points of law by either the licensing justices, magistrates' court or by the Crown Court sitting in its appellate capacity in licensing cases. The power to state a case only exists if there is specific statutory provision for it. Such a provision is to be found in s 111 of the Magistrates' Courts Act 1980. The effect of this is that in most licensing hearings before the justices there is power to state a case. However, there is no power for the Crown Court to state a case in the majority of licensing cases heard by it: see LA64, s 23(3), nor for magistrates to do so if their decision is interlocutory in nature.
Judicial review will be appropriate in the following cases:
(1) to challenge a decision of the Crown Court;
(2) to challenge an interlocutory decision made by the justices.

1 Applications by way of case stated

Any person who was a party to any proceedings before a magistrates' court or is aggrieved by the final order of the court may question the proceeding on the ground that it is wrong in law or is in excess of jurisdiction by applying for a case to be stated for the consideration of the High Court. The application must be made within twenty-one days after the day on which the decision was given. Once the application is made any right of appeal to the Crown Court is lost. The procedure is to be found in Rules 70–81 of the Magistrates' Courts Rules 1981 (SI No 552) and in Orders 56 and 57 RSC.

Unlike an application for judicial review there is no need to seek leave. However the justices may, if they consider the application frivolous, refuse to state a case. The hearing is before the Divisional Court which has the power to reverse, affirm or amend the determination of the magistrates' court or remit the matter to the justices.

There is a discretion to award costs.

2 Applications for judicial review

The procedure is governed by Order 53 RSC, the substantive law is common law. A major matter which has to be investigated is whether the would-be applicant has exhausted his remedies before making the application. Judicial review will not normally be granted where another avenue of appeal exists which has not been used (*R v Epping and Harlow General Commissioners Ex parte Goldstraw* [1983] 3 All ER 257 CA).

The party making the application will be a person who has failed in his application or has succeeded subject to conditions or who has failed successfully to object. The respondent will be the relevant tribunal—most often the justices but in some cases the Crown Court sitting at XYZ or the Gaming Board.

(a) The grounds on which judicial review can be granted

(1) Want or excess of jurisdiction.

(2) Where there is an error of law on the face of the record.

(3) Breach of the rules of natural justice. The basic principle on which the Divisional Court acts is to ask itself whether the tribunal has acted fairly. Examples of cases in the licensing field are: *R v Gaming Board for Great Britain Ex parte Benaim and Khanda* (1970) 2 QB 417 [1970] 2 All ER 528 CA and *R v Bath Licensing Justices Ex parte Cooper* [1989] 2 All ER 897 and *R v Crown Court at Bristol Ex parte Cooper* [1990] 2 All ER 193.

(4) Unreasonableness. This basis is commonly known as 'the Wednesbury principle' as it is based on the decision in *Associated Provincial Picture Houses Ltd v Wednesbury Corporation* [1948] 1 KB 223, [1947] 2 All ER 680. The court asks itself whether a tribunal properly directing itself on the law and acting reasonably could have reached the decision under review.

The grant of judicial review is discretionary. There is no right to it; however if the applicant can bring his case within the above headings and has followed the correct procedure he will usually be granted relief.

(b) The types of relief available

(1) Certiorari: this order brings up into the High Court the decision of an inferior tribunal and quashes it. On the granting of this order the court has power to send the case back to the tribunal with a direction to reconsider it and to reach a decision by applying the court's judgment. This form of relief is the most commonly sought in licensing cases.
(2) Prohibition: this order restrains an inferior tribunal from acting outside its jurisdiction.
(3) Mandamus: this order compels an inferior tribunal to carry out its function.

In addition it is possible to be awarded damages, a declaration and an injunction. Under Order 53.8 of the RSC it is possible to apply for a variety of interlocutory orders.

(c) Procedure

In all cases there must first be an application for leave. This must be made promptly, ie as soon as practicable or in any event within three months from the date of the matter complained of. Although the court has power to extend this period it is now not uncommon for the court to refuse to hear an application even if it has been made within the three-month period on the basis that it was not made promptly. The prudent approach must be to apply as soon as possible after the relevant hearing.

The application for leave is made initially in writing using form 86A. The applicant must state:

(1) his name and description;
(2) the relief sought and the grounds upon which it is sought;
(3) the name and address of the applicant's solicitors;
(4) the applicant's address for service.

The form must be filed with an affidavit verifying the facts relied on. It may request an expedited hearing if there is good reason. The application is usually determined by a judge without an oral hearing, although it is possible to request such a hearing on form 86A.

The application is normally made ex parte. The judge should grant leave if it is clear that there is a point fit for further investigation on a full inter partes basis. If the judge is satisfied that there is no arguable case he should dismiss the application. If he is in real doubt he should invite the applicant and the proposed respondent to make short oral representations to him in order to make his decision. When leave has been granted ex parte a respondent can apply for the leave to be discharged.

Assuming however that leave has been granted the applicant within fourteen days of the grant of leave must serve an originating motion and a copy of the affidavit in support of his application for leave on all parties directly affected and enter the motion. The respondent must, within fifty-six days of service, file any affidavits on which he will rely.

The hearing is usually in open court before a single QB judge. There is a right of appeal against the decision to the Court of Appeal. There is a general discretion as to costs.

If the application is refused or conditionally granted and there has been no oral hearing it can be renewed (usually to a single judge sitting in open court). The application for renewal is in form 86B and must be made within ten days of service of the decision. Where leave is refused after a hearing (whether on the initial application for leave or on a renewed application) a further application may be made to the Court of Appeal within seven days. If the Court of Appeal allows the appeal and grants leave it usually remits the case to a single judge for the substantive hearing. There is no appeal from a refusal of the Court of Appeal to grant leave.

Appendices

1   Notice of application for justices' licence

2   Notice of application for transfer of justices' licence

3   Application for restaurant certificate (licensed premises)

4   Application for special hours certificate

5   Notice of appeal to the Crown Court

6   Application for grant of a bookmaker's permit by a company

7   Application for grant of betting office licence

8   Application for renewal of betting office licence

9   Application for grant of gaming club licence

10   Application for renewal of gaming club licence

11   Specified areas for 'hard' gaming

12   Application for the (issue) (renewal) (variation) of club registration certificate

13   Application for grant of permit under s 34 of the Gaming Act 1968

Appendix 1: Notice of application for justices' licence

To the Clerk to the Licensing Justices for the Licensing District of Barchester.
To the Chief Constable of

To the proper officer of the district council for the district of

To   , as fire authority.

TAKE NOTICE that I, John Bull, of 1 King Street, Barchester, in the County of Barset, who have during the past six months carried on the trade or calling of a grocer, propose to apply at the licensing sessions to be held at the Town Hall, High Street, Barchester aforesaid, on the 1st day of June, 199 , at 10.30 am, for the grant to me of a new justices' licence authorising me to sell intoxicating liquor of all descriptions by retail for consumption either on or off the premises situate at No 2 Station Approach, Barchester, and to be known as the 'Swan of Barset'. A plan of the said premises has been deposited with the Clerk to the Justices with this notice. The owner of the said premises is Jack Spratt, of 2 Kensington Arcade, London, SW1.
    Dated the   day of   199

Signed: Wills and Seal,
Solicitors, of 88 Queen's Hill, Barchester
(authorised agents for the applicant)

Appendix 2: Notice of application for transfer of justices' licence

To the holder of the undermentioned licence,
To the Clerk to the Licensing Justices for the Licensing District of
To the Chief Officer of Police
To the Proper Officer of the   Council

I, JOHN BULL who has resided for the past six months at 1 King Street, Barchester in the County of Barset and carried on the trade or calling during the aforesaid period of six months of Grocer HEREBY GIVE YOU NOTICE that it is my intention to apply at the Licensing Sessions for the Licensing District of Barchester to be held at The Town Hall, High Street, Barchester, aforesaid on Monday the 1st day of June 199 at 10.30 am for the TRANSFER to me of the Justices' Licence for the sale by retail of any intoxicating liquor which may be sold for consumption on/off the premises situate at   and known as   now held by the said

GIVEN UNDER MY HAND this   day of   199 .

Appendix 3: Application for restaurant certificate (licensed premises)

To the Clerk to the Licensing Justices for the Licensing District of Barchester.
To the Chief Constable of

TAKE NOTICE that I, George Mynehost of the Old White Horse, 2 Station Street, Barchester intend to apply at the transfer sessions to be held at
on the   day of   199 for a certificate that the licensing justices for the said   are satisfied that the licensed premises known as the Old White Horse, situated at 2 Station Street, Barchester, in the said   are structurally adapted and bona fide intended to be used for the purpose of habitually providing for the accommodation of persons frequenting the premises substantial refreshment to which the sale and supply of intoxicating liquor is ancillary.
   AND FURTHER TAKE NOTICE that if such certificate is granted both paragraphs of section 68 of the Licensing Act 1964 will apply to the said premises from the   day of   next.
   Dated the   day of   199

Signed: George Mynehost

Appendix 4: Application for special hours certificate

To the Chief Constable of
To the Clerk to the Licensing Justices for the Licensing District of Barchester.

TAKE NOTICE that I, John Bull, of 1 King Street, Barchester intend to apply to the said Licensing Justices at the transfer sessions to be held on   at   for a special hours certificate under section 77 of the Licensing Act 1964 for the part mentioned below of the licensed premises situated at 2 Station Approach, Barchester, and known as the 'Swan of Barset' (that is to say   ).
   AND FURTHER TAKE NOTICE that if such a certificate is granted section 76 of the said Act will apply to the said part from the   day of   199

Signed: Wills and Seal,
Solicitors, of 88 Queen's Hill, Barchester
(authorised agents for the applicant)

Appendix 5: Notice of appeal to the Crown Court (against refusal to grant new on-licence)

To the Clerk to the Licensing Justices for the Licensing District of Barchester.
To George Mynehost, of the Old White Horse, Station Street, Barchester.

TAKE NOTICE that I, John Bull, of 1 King Street, Barchester, intend to appeal to the Crown Court pursuant to section 21 of the Licensing Act 1964 against a decision of the said licensing justices given at their transfer sessions on 1 June, 199 , whereby they refused to grant to me a new justices' licence for the sale of intoxicating liquor of all descriptions by retail for consumption on or off the premises situate at 2 Station Approach, Barchester, and to be known as 'The Swan of Barset'.

AND TAKE NOTICE THAT THE GROUNDS OF MY APPEAL are:
(a) that the said decision was against the weight of the evidence;
(b) that there were no or no sufficient reasons why the said licence should not have been granted;
(c) that the said licence was and is required to meet a public need;
(d) that the said decision was wrong and ought to be reversed.

(*or as the case may be*)

Signed: John Bull

Dated this   day of   199
Note The notice is given to the justices' clerk and any person who appeared and objected to the grant.

Appendix 6: Application for grant of a bookmaker's permit by a company (See Schedule to Betting (Licensing) Regulations 1960 SI No 1701, as amended)

To the Clerk to the Betting Licensing Committee for the Petty Sessional Division of Barchester in the County of Barset.

I, Thomas Atkins, duly authorised in that behalf by Barchester Bookmakers Limited hereby apply for and on behalf of the said Company for a bookmaker's permit and declare as follows:
That the said company is incorporated in Great Britain and has its registered office at   .
That the names and addresses of the directors and secretary of the said company and of the persons in accordance with whose directions or instructions the directors therefore are accustomed to act are as follows:
(*indicate who are the directors and who is the secretary*).

That the said company has not during the twelve months immediately preceding the date of this application been refused the grant or renewal of a bookmaker's permit or betting agency permit save as follows: (*insert details of refusals*).

That the said company has not been the holder of a bookmaker's permit or betting agency permit which has been forfeited and cancelled save as follows: (*insert details of cancellations*).

Dated this   day of   199 .

Signed: T Atkins,
Company Secretary,
Barchester Bookmakers Ltd.

Note (a)   (Two references as to the character of each director and of each person in accordance with whose directions or instructions the directors are accustomed to act, are to be provided in the following form).

I,   of (description) have known   of   for a period of   years and am of the opinion that he would be a fit and proper person to be the holder of a bookmaker's permit. I am not related to him.

Dated this   day of   199 .

Note (b)   For its adaptation to other circumstances see the Regulations referred to above.

Appendix 7: Application for grant of betting office licence (See Schedule to Betting (Licensing) Regulations 1960, SI No 1701, as amended)

To the Clerk to the Betting Licensing Committee for the Petty Sessional Division of Barchester in the County of Barset.

I, Thomas Atkins, of   (duly authorised in that behalf by Barchester Bookmakers Limited) hereby apply for and on behalf of the said Company for a betting office licence in respect of the shop premises situate at No 2 Grand Parade, Barchester, aforesaid, a plan whereof, sufficient to show the layout and location of the said premises and the means of access thereto, is appended hereto, and declare as follows:

That the said Company is the holder of a bookmaker's permit last renewed on the   day of   199   by (*insert appropriate authority*).

Dated the   day of   199 .

Signed: T Atkins,
Company Secretary,
Barchester Bookmakers Ltd.

Note   The above form is appropriate where application is made on behalf of a company which holds a bookmaker's permit. For its adaptation to other circumstances see the regulations referred to above.

Appendix 8: Application for renewal of betting office licence (See Schedule to Betting (Licensing) Regulations 1960, SI No 1701, as amended.)

To the Clerk to the Betting Licensing Committee for the Petty Sessional Division of Barchester in the County of Barset.

I, Thomas Atkins (duly authorised in that behalf by Barchester Bookmakers Limited), hereby apply for and on behalf of the said Company for the renewal of the betting office licence in respect of the betting office premises situate at No 2 Grand Parade, Barchester aforesaid last renewed on the   day of 199 , and declare as follows:

(*a*) That the said Company is the holder of a bookmaker's permit last renewed on the   day of   199 by (*insert appropriate authority*);

(*b*) That there has been no change in the layout of the said premises and the means of access thereto since the last renewal of the said licence.

    Dated the   day of   199

                              Signed: T Atkins,
                              Company Secretary,
                              Barchester Bookmakers Limited.

Note This form is applicable where application is made on behalf of a company which holds a bookmaker's permit, and there has been no change in the layout and means of access. For its adaptation to other circumstances, see the regulations referred to above.

Appendix 9: Application for grant of gaming club licence (See GCLR69, Sched 2)

GAMING ACT 1968

To the Clerk to the Gaming Licensing Committee for the Petty Sessions area of Barchester in the County of Barset.

Barset Casinos Limited of 1 High Street, Barchester aforesaid, hereby applies for a licence under the Gaming Act 1968 in respect of the premises shown on the plan attached hereto and consisting of the former Cinema premises, formerly known as the Grand Cinema, situate at No 2 High Street, Barchester aforesaid.

The premises are intended to be used for the purposes of the club named as follows: The Swan of Barset Bingo Club, whose principal purpose is intended to be: social intercourse and the playing of bingo.

It is intended that the licence should be granted subject to the following restrictions under paragraphs 24 and 25 of Schedule 2 to the Act:

as to hours of gaming: (*as required*)

as to parts of the premises to be used for gaming: (*as the case may be*)

as to the kinds of games to be played (apart from slot-machines and gaming for small prizes): Bingo only

If this application is granted it is desired that a direction should be given under section 32 of the Act that the maximum number of machines (to which Part III of the Act applies) to be available for gaming shall be three (*or as the case may be a number more than two*). The names and addresses of the Directors and Secretary of the applicant company are as follows:

William Brewer of 1 Fog Lane, Barchester; Director.
Jan Stewer of 2 Pitt Street, Barchester; Director.
Peter Davey of 5 King Street, Barchester; Director.
Daniel Widden of 6 Queen Street, Barchester; Director.
Harold Hawke of 7 Old Street, Barchester; Secretary.

A copy of the relevant certificate of consent issued by the Gaming Board of Great Britain dated the   day of   199   and
                                        numbered
is attached. It is limited to a bingo club licence.

Dated the   day of   199

Signed: Harold Hawke,
Company Secretary,
Barset Casinos Limited.

Note

(*a*) This form is applicable where application is made on behalf of a company, and the club is to be one for bingo only. For its adaptation to other circumstances, see GCLR69.

(*b*) The reference to a direction under s 32 is in connection with the power conferred by that section on the justices to authorise the installation on the club premises of more than two gaming machines to be used for small prizes. This power may be exercised on any application to grant or renew a licence.

Appendix 10: Application for renewal of gaming club licence (See GCLR69, Sched 2)

GAMING ACT 1968
To the Clerk to the Gaming Licensing Committee for the Petty Sessions area of Barchester in the County of Barset.

Barset Casinos Limited of No 1 High Street, Barchester aforesaid, hereby applies for the renewal of the licence under the Gaming Act 1968 which was last renewed on the   day of   199 , in respect of the premises consisting of the former Cinema premises, formerly known as the Grand Cinema, now known as the Swan of Barset Bingo Club, situate at the following address: No 2 High Street, Barchester aforesaid.

There has been no change in the premises or their layout or in the means of access to the premises since the licence was last renewed. The premises are used for the purposes of the club named as follows: The Swan of Barset Bingo Club, whose principal purpose is: social intercourse and the playing of bingo. The licence was last renewed subject to the following restrictions: (*as the case may be*); and it is proposed that they be re-imposed (*or as the case may be*). If this application is granted it is desired that a direction should be given under section 32 of the Act that the maximum number of machines (to which Part III of the Act applies) to be available for gaming shall be three (*or as the case may be; a number more than two*).

The names and addresses of the Directors and Secretary of the applicant company are as follows:

William Brewer of 1 Fog Lane, Barchester; Director.

Jan Stewer of 2 Pitt Street, Barchester; Director.

Peter Davey of 5 King Street, Barchester; Director.

Daniel Widden of 6 Queen Street, Barchester; Director.

Harold Hawke of 7 Old Street, Barchester; Secretary.

The relevant certificate of consent issued by the Gaming Board of Great Britain which is dated   and numbered   is limited to a bingo club licence.

Signed: Harold Hawke,
Company Secretary,
Barset Casinos Limited.

Note

(*a*) This form is applicable where application is made on behalf of a company which holds a licence which has been renewed, and where there has been no change in the layout and means of access and the club is for bingo only. For its adaptation to other circumstances, see GCLR69.

(*b*) The reference to a direction under s 32 is in connection with the power conferred by that section on the justices to authorise the installation on club premises of more than two gaming machines to be used for small prizes. This power may be exercised on any application to grant or renew a licence.

Appendix 11: Specified areas for 'hard' gaming

Under the Gaming Clubs (Permitted Areas) Regulations 1971 (SI No 1538), the justices must refuse to grant or renew a licence for 'hard' gaming where the licence is to be in respect of premises outside the specified areas. The specified areas are:

(*a*) every county borough the area of which was shown as having an estimated population of 125,000 or more in any of the annual estimates made by the Registrar General and published between 1 December 1970 and 1 October 1973, and

(*b*) the following places:

County Boroughs:	Great Yarmouth	
	Southport	
	Torbay	
Non-County Boroughs:	Hove	Ramsgate
	Lytham St Annes	Ryde
	Margate	Scarborough
Urban Districts:	Sandown—Shanklin	
London Boroughs:	Royal Borough of Kensington and Chelsea	
	City of Westminster	

That part of the London Borough of Camden which is within the area specified in the Licensing (Metropolitan Special Hours Area) Order 1961.

Note Although s 1(10) of the Local Government Act 1972 has abolished the old local government areas, such as urban districts etc, the areas set out above continue as 'specified areas' for the purposes of the regulations referred to.

Appendix 12: Application for the (issue) (renewal) (variation) of club registration certificate (Licensing Act 1964)

APPLICATION [1] IS HEREBY MADE to the   Magistrates' Court for the (Issue) (Renewal) (Variation) of a REGISTRATION CERTIFICATE under the above Act.

1. Name of Club
2. Objects of Club
3. Address of Club

at which address is kept a list of the names and addresses of the members.

I, the undersigned [Chairman] [Secretary] of the Club, hereby state as follows:—

4. Under the rules of the Club persons may not be admitted to membership, or be admitted as candidates for membership to any of the privileges of membership, without an interval of at least two days between their nomination or application for membership and their admission; and persons becoming members without prior nomination or application may not be admitted to the privileges of membership without an interval of at least two days between their becoming members and their admission.

The Club is established and conducted in good faith as a Club, and has not less than twenty-five members; and intoxicating liquor is not supplied, or intended to be supplied, to members on the premises otherwise than by or on behalf of the Club; and the purchase for the Club, and the supply by the Club, of intoxicating liquor (so far as not managed by the Club in general meeting or otherwise by the general body of members) is managed by an elective committee, as defined in the Seventh Schedule to the above Act.

No arrangements are, or are intended, to be made—

(a) for any person to receive at the expense of the Club any commission, percentage or similar payment on or with reference to purchases of intoxicating liquor by the Club; or

(b) for any person directly or indirectly to derive any pecuniary benefit from the supply of intoxicating liquor by or on behalf of the Club to members or guests, apart from any benefit accruing to the Club as a whole and apart also from any benefit which a person derives indirectly by reason of the supply giving rise or contributing to a general gain from the carrying on of the Club.

The Club is, therefore, qualified under subsections (1) and (2) of section forty-one of the above Act to receive a Registration Certificate for the premises, or will be so qualified if, as regards any provision of the rules specified in this application, the Court sees fit to give a direction under section 42 (2) of the above Act.

5. The names and addresses of the members of the committee having the general management of the affairs of the Club are [as follows:—] [incorporated in a document annexed hereto].

6. The names and addresses of the members of the committee concerned with the purchase for the Club or with the supply by the Club of intoxicating liquor are [as follows:—] [incorporated in a document annexed hereto].

7. The names and addresses of other officers of the Club are [as follows:—] [incorporated in a document annexed hereto].

8. [[The rules of the Club] [The changes in the rules of the Club [2] made since the last application for the issue or renewal or variation of a Registration Certificate] are incorporated in a document annexed hereto].

[No changes in the rules of the Club have been made since the last application for the issue or renewal or variation of a Registration Certificate].

9. The premises for which the [issue] [renewal] [variation] of (a) (the) Registration Certificate is sought are—

10. The last-named premises are or are to be occupied by and habitually used for the purposes of the Club and are or are to be open to members at the following times:—

And the following hours are fixed by or under the rules of the Club as the permitted hours for the supply of intoxicating liquor there:—

Weekdays—

Sundays, Christmas Day and Good Friday –

11. The interest held by or in trust for the Club in the last-named premises is—[3]

[The name and address of any person to whom payment is or is to be made for rent under lease or otherwise for the use of the premises is—]

12. Particulars of any property not comprised in paragraph 9 above which is or is to be used for the purposes of the Club and not held by or in trust for the Club absolutely, and the name and address of any person to whom payment is or is to be made for the use of that property, are [4] [as follows:—] [incorporated in a document annexed hereto].

13. Particulars of any liability of the Club in respect of the principal or interest of moneys borrowed by the Club or charged on property held by or in trust for the Club, including the name and address of the person to whom payment is or is to be made on account of that principal or interest, are [5] [as follows:—] [incorporated in a document annexed hereto].

14. Particulars of any liability of the Club or of a trustee for the Club in respect of which any person has given any guarantee or provided any security,

together with particulars of the guarantee or security given or provided, including the name and address of the person giving or providing it, are [6] [as follows:—] [incorporated in a document annexed hereto].

15. Particulars of any premises not comprised in paragraph 9 above which have within the preceding twelve months been occupied and habitually used for the purposes of the Club and the interest then held by or in trust for the Club in those premises and, if it was a leasehold interest or if the Club had no interest, the name and address of any person to whom payment was made of rent under the lease or otherwise for the use of the premises are [7] [as follows:—] [incorporated in a document annexed hereto].

16. [It is requested that the Registration Certificate be renewed for a period of   years.] [8]

17. The Club is [not] a registered society within the meaning of the Industrial and Provident Societies Act 1893, or the Friendly Societies Act 1896.

Dated the   day of   19   .

Signed:
[*Chairman*] [*Secretary*] of the Club.

Notes

(1) This form of Application should be used for either the issue or renewal of a Registration Certificate or the renewal or variation of a Registration Certificate in respect of different, additional or enlarged premises. Identify premises at paragraph 9 stating any changes to the premises since the Certificate was issued or last renewed. This Application must be made by lodging with the Clerk to the Justices (or the Clerk to the Metropolitan Stipendiary Court, as the case may be) a sufficient number of copies (normally three) to enable him to retain one copy and send a copy each to any chief officer of police concerned and to the clerk of any local authority concerned.

In addition to this, a new Club (that is to say, a Club applying for its first Registration Certificate) or a Club applying for renewal or variation of a Registration Certificate in respect of different, additional or enlarged premises, must give public notice of the Application (Licensing Act 1964, 6th Schedule, paragraph 5.) A form of public notice (Licensing 4) is obtainable from the Publishers.

(2) If the Application is for the renewal of a Registration Certificate, only the changes in the rules made since the last Application need be annexed.

(3) 'Freehold';   'Leasehold'; 'None'; as the case may be.

(4), (5), (6) 'No property' or 'No liability'; if such be the case. An Application for renewal of a Registration Certificate may give the particulars required by reference to the changes (if any) since the last Application.

(7) 'No premises' if such be the case.

Where the interest held by or in trust for the Club in any land of which particulars are required under paragraphs 11, 12, 13, 14 or 15 of the Application is or was a leasehold interest, and the rent under the lease is not or was not paid by the Club or the trustees for the Club, the Application shall state the name and address of the person by whom it is or was paid. (Licens-

      } ing Act 1964, 5th Schedule, para-
      } graph 8).

(8) If the Application is for a second renewal of a Registration Certificate,
state the number of years (not exceeding ten) for which renewal is requested;
otherwise delete this paragraph.

Reproduced with the kind permission of The Solicitors' Law Stationery
Society plc.

Appendix 13: Application for grant of permit under s 34 of the Gaming Act 1968

To the Clerk to the Licensing Justices for the Licensing District of Barchester.

I, John Bull of 1 King Street, Barchester, being the holder of a Justices' On
Licence (other than a Part IV Licence) in respect of premises situate at
and known as   hereby apply for the grant of a Permit under Section 34
of the Gaming Act 1968 in respect of the said premises for   amusement
machines with prizes.
    Dated this   day of   199 .

Signed: John Bull.

Note In the case of premises holding a part IV Licence application is made to
the Local Authority and this form should be adjusted accordingly.

Index